THE
MEDITERRANEAN DIET COOKBOOK

A MEDITERRANEAN DIET COOKBOOK WITH 150 HEALTHY MEDITERRANEAN DIET RECIPES

CONTENTS

Chapter 7: Grains and Pastas   85

Chapter 11: Vegetable Dishes

Chapter 12: Desserts

INTRODUCTION

L iving well is the best revenge. If the Mediterranean diet could be summed up in one sentence, that would be it. Living well is simply a way of life for Mediterraneans, where eating a diet that is based on vegetables, grains, and legumes, with small amounts of dairy, eggs, and poultry, and even smaller amounts of red meat is the norm. But so too is dining with friends and getting regular physical activity. If a sunny trip to Greece or Italy or the south of France appeals to you, this diet will take you there in spirit.

If you visit the region, you will find there is no single "Mediterranean diet" that all inhabitants of countries as disparate as France, Italy, Spain, Turkey, Greece, and Israel follow, but there is a common thread. Technically speaking, their diet is high in monounsaturated fatty acids, fiber, and antioxidants, and low in saturated fat.

In 1993, the concept of a Mediterranean diet was introduced by Oldways, the Harvard School of Public Health, and the World Health Organization. The diet is based on research that began with Dr. Ancel Keys, who conducted a fifteen-year study of seven countries, which began in 1958. Numerous studies followed, and the results were impressive. Those in Mediterranean countries suffered from less heart disease and were generally healthier. The studies seemed to prove that *la cucina povera* was actually healthier than more modern diets in more industrialized parts of the world.

The Mediterranean diet is based on the traditional foods eaten by people living in the Mediterranean region, especially in Crete. If you remember the advice "eat like your ancestors," you'll be on the right track. Your ancestors did not eat soft drinks, processed food, or fast food, and neither should you.

This diet is not specifically for weight loss but for overall health; however, it is possible to lose weight on the diet, especially if your usual eating habits align more with the traditional American diet of processed foods and bad fats. The Mediterranean diet is particularly good for heart health, reducing the incidence of cancer and cancer mortality, and reducing the incidence of Parkinson's and Alzheimer's diseases, according to the Mayo Clinic. *U.S. News & World Report* ranks the Mediterranean diet highly in the categories of Best Diets Overall, Best Diets for Healthy Eating, and Easiest Diet to Follow.

Starting at the base, here are the basic guidelines for the Mediterranean Diet Pyramid:

- Every meal should be based on fruits, vegetable, grains (mostly whole), olive oil, beans, nuts, legumes, seeds, herbs, and spices.
- Fish and seafood should be consumed often, at least two times a week.
- Cheese and yogurt are allowed in moderation, daily to weekly.
- Poultry and eggs are allowed in moderate portions, every two days or weekly.
- Meats and sweets should be eaten rarely.
- Drinking water is encouraged, and wine is allowed, especially red wine, in moderation.
- Physicall activity is encouraged, as is enjoying meals with others.

While eating habits and diets vary greatly in the Mediterranean, research shows that the people who live in this region tend to eat a diet high in fat, yet they have a much lower incidence of cardiovascular disease and cancer than people in other parts of the world.

On the Mediterranean diet there are no calories to count, no specifically forbidden foods or bizarre food combinations. If you want to lose weight, you will have to limit calories and unhealthful saturated fat and, of course, exercise more. But the diet itself is as simple as can be.

Use the pyramid and guidelines, be inspired by the recipes, live well, and be healthy.

WHAT IS THE MEDITERRANEAN DIET?

U nlike many diets, the Mediterranean diet isn't actually a diet at all, at least not in the traditional you-can't-eat-that sense. It's more of a guideline for living a long, healthy, happy life. You may have to make some modifications to your lifestyle and your way of thinking, but you're not going to need to give up a single thing—except for bad health and unsightly body fat. In exchange, you'll need to eat plenty of foods that taste delicious, find some vigorous activities that you enjoy, and spend more time with your friends and family. Sound good? If so, then this may just be the "diet" that you've been searching for!

What Makes the Mediterranean Diet Different From Other Diets?

Excellent question. For the last several decades, the prevailing opinion among health experts has been that the key to maintaining a healthful weight and avoiding disease is eating a diet low in carbohydrates and fat. Unfortunately, this theory isn't backed by science. Your body needs healthful fats and good carbs to produce energy and fight disease, and your brain needs them to function optimally, too.

The Foods

The Mediterranean diet has a food pyramid that allows any kind of food but places them in a hierarchical order. Here, fattier meats and sweets are at the top of the pyramid, to be consumed in moderation. Foods high in nutrients, healthful carbs, and essential fats are at the bottom of the pyramid, as main components of every meal. These healthful foods include fresh fruits and vegetables, whole grains, legumes, olive oil, herbs, and spices.

The second-largest layer of the pyramid consists of fish and seafood, which you should eat at least twice weekly. The third layer is beneath meats and sweets and is composed of poultry, eggs, cheese, and yogurt, which should be eaten moderately on a daily or weekly basis. In addition to the following the food pyramid, you should consume a healthful supply of water and a moderate amount of wine.

The Lifestyle

Perhaps what really sets the Mediterranean diet apart is the fact that their pyramid is built atop a base that has nothing to do with nutrition. Instead, the basis for a healthy life includes being physically active and sharing meals based upon the food pyramid with other people whom you care about and enjoy spending time with. It's a holistic approach that teaches that to be truly healthy and happy, you need to feed your mind and your spirit as well as your body.

Eat Your Way to Better Health and Happiness

The Mediterranean diet concept and illustrative pyramid were introduced in 1993, based on the eating habits of Greeks and Italians who lived along the Mediterranean Sea in the early 1960s. These people enjoyed extraordinarily good physical and mental health in comparison to Western eaters, and they lived longer, too. So what are the benefits of the Mediterranean diet? Here are just a few.

Avoid Illness and Disease

Fresh fruits and veggies have an enormous amount of vitamins, nutrients, phytonutrients, and antioxidants that help your body fight disease. Because the Mediterranean diet encourages you to eat a wide variety of produce as part of every meal and snack, your body will get the full spectrum of nutrients that it needs to function properly.

Antioxidants in produce fight off free radicals that cause all kinds of damage, including wrinkles and other signs of aging, dull hair, poor skin, heart disease, eye disease, and even cancer. Free radicals are the result of respiration, environmental pollutants, and some are even created by your body in order to carry out toxic cells, but too many are disastrous. Antioxidants neutralize free radicals before they can cause further damage.

Consume Plenty of Fiber

There are two basic types of fiber: soluble and insoluble. The insoluble fiber in fresh produce, legumes, and nuts acts like a broom and sweeps all of the accumulated food and toxins from your digestive tract so that it may function optimally. Soluble fiber binds with fatty acids and helps slow down sugar (glucose) absorption so that you have a steady supply of energy. It also helps lower bad cholesterol, therefore promoting heart health, which moves us right along to the next benefit of the Mediterranean diet.

Keep Your Heart and Veins Healthy

The Mediterranean diet promotes cardiovascular health in a variety of ways. The soluble fiber that we've already discussed helps lower bad cholesterol, and the abundance of antioxidants helps prevent plaque buildup caused free radicals. The American Heart Association promotes consumption of foods rich in omega-3s as a great way to promote cardiovascular health. These essential fatty acids help lower triglycerides and bad cholesterol and are even linked to healthful blood pressure. If you've already experienced a heart attack, research shows that increasing your omega-3 intake can reduce the risk of a repeat episode.

Improve Mood and Cognitive Function

Studies have recently linked Alzheimer's disease to insulin resistance so surely that the disease is now being referred to as type 3 diabetes. A diet that promotes a steady supply of foods with a low glycemic load is a great way to prevent diet-related insulin resistance and is the epitome of what the Mediterranean diet teaches.

Your brain also requires a significant amount of essential omega-3 fatty acids found in fatty fish, olive oil, and many plants in order to function properly. Since your body can't make these, it's imperative that you get them from your diet. In addition to all of their other health benefits, omega-3s have been shown to help you think clearly and avoid depression and other anxiety-related conditions.

Support Weight Loss

Weight loss is more of a side effect of healthful eating than a goal of following the Mediterranean diet, though that's what may attract you to it initially. Because one of the primary characteristics of the lifestyle is decreased stress via the pursuit of personal happiness, drastically reducing caloric intake isn't a concept that's promoted. However, changing your eating style to conform to the Mediterranean lifestyle will automatically put you on the path to a leaner, happier you because you're not eating a ton of fatty, calorie-dense junk.

Now that you're familiar with the Mediterranean diet, let's get on to the recipes. You're truly not going to believe how scrumptious these are, and when you taste them, you're going to wonder what took you so long to try them. *Mangia bene!*

2

BREAKFASTS

- Apple and Tahini Toast
- Banana Corn Cakes
- Cinnamon Bulgur with Berries
- Fresh Veggie Frittata
- Garlic Scrambled Eggs with Basil
- Greek Eggs and Potatoes
- Honey and Avocado Smoothie
- Peach and Walnut Breakfast Salad
- Peachy Green Smoothie
- Savory Breakfast Oats
- Scrambled Eggs with Feta and Olives
- Spanish Tuna Tortilla with Roasted Peppers
- Spiced Scrambled Eggs

Apple and Tahini Toast

Tahini is a paste made from sesame seeds, and is high in vitamins B1, B2, B3, B5, and B15. Similar to peanut butter, it's often found in dips such as hummus. In some countries, it is commonly served for breakfast with toast.

- 2 tablespoons tahini
- 2 slices whole-wheat bread, toasted
- 1 small apple of your choice, cored and thinly sliced
- 1 teaspoon honey

Spread the tahini on the toasted bread.

Lay the apples on the bread and drizzle with honey.

Serve immediately.

Serves 1.

Banana Corn Cakes

While you may think of bananas as a tropical fruit, they have been grown in the Mediterranean region for centuries. Bananas are a good source of dietary fiber, vitamin C, potassium, and manganese. In these easy-to-make corn cakes, they add moisture and sweetness.

- 1/2 cup yellow cornmeal
- 1/4 cup flour
- 2 small ripe bananas, peeled and mashed
- 1 large egg
- 2 tablespoons milk
- 1/2 teaspoon baking powder
- 1/4–1/2 teaspoon ground chipotle chili
- 1/4 teaspoon sea salt
- 1/4 teaspoon ground cinnamon
- 1 tablespoon olive oil

Combine all ingredients except for the oil in a large bowl, and mix well until smooth.

Heat a cast-iron or nonstick skillet over medium-high heat.

Add the olive oil and drop the batter into the skillet using a spoon. Avoid letting the cakes touch.

Cook until the bottoms are golden brown, then flip.

Cakes are done when golden brown on both sides. Serve immediately.

Serves 2.

Cinnamon Bulgur with Berries

Bulgur is easy to cook and full of fiber, but it is also low in fat and calories. While commonly used in more savory dishes, it makes a lovely hot breakfast, especially when paired with cinnamon and berries. Serve this cereal dish instead of oatmeal on a chilly morning.

- 1/2 cup medium-grain bulgur wheat
- 1 cup water
- Pinch sea salt
- 1/4 cup milk
- 1 teaspoon pure vanilla extract
- 1/4 teaspoon ground cinnamon
- 1 cup fresh berries of your choice

Put the bulgur in a medium saucepan with the water and sea salt, and bring to a boil.

Cover, remove from heat, and let stand for 10 minutes until water is absorbed.

Stir in the milk, vanilla, and cinnamon until fully incorporated.

Divide between 2 bowls and top with the fresh berries to serve.

Serves 2.

Fresh Veggie Frittata

You can use whatever ingredients you have for this recipe—grilled or roasted vegetables add great depth of flavor, as well as nutrition.

- 3 large eggs
- 1 teaspoon almond milk
- 1 tablespoon olive oil
- 1 handful baby spinach leaves
- 1/2 baby eggplant, peeled and diced
- 1/4 small red bell pepper, chopped
- Sea salt and freshly ground pepper, to taste
- 1 ounce crumbled goat cheese

Preheat the broiler.

Beat the eggs with the almond milk until just combined.

Heat a small nonstick, broiler-proof skillet over medium-high heat. Add the olive oil, followed by the eggs.

Spread the spinach on top of the egg mixture in an even layer and top with the rest of the veggies.

Reduce heat to medium and season with sea salt and freshly ground pepper to taste. Allow the eggs and vegetables to cook 3–5 minutes until the bottom half of the eggs are firm and vegetables are tender.

Top with the crumbled goat cheese and place on middle rack under the broiler, and then cook another 3–5 minutes until the eggs are firm in the middle and the cheese has melted.

Slice into wedges and serve immediately.

Serves 1.

Garlic Scrambled Eggs with Basil

This version of scrambled eggs is anything but bland. Basil and garlic add Mediterranean flavor to this breakfast staple. Serve with whole-grain toast or a fruit and nut muffin.

- 4 large eggs
- 2 tablespoons finely chopped fresh basil
- 2 tablespoons grated Gruyère cheese

- 1 tablespoon cream
- 1 tablespoon olive oil
- 2 cloves garlic, minced
- Sea salt and freshly ground pepper, to taste

In a large bowl, beat together the eggs, basil, cheese, and cream with a whisk until just combined.

Heat the oil in a large, heavy nonstick skillet over medium-low heat. Add the garlic and cook until golden, about 1 minute.

Pour the egg mixture into the skillet over the garlic. Work the eggs continuously and cook until fluffy and soft.

Season with sea salt and freshly ground pepper to taste.

Divide between 2 plates and serve immediately.

Serves 2.

Greek Eggs and Potatoes

Eggs get a nutritional and flavor boost from fresh tomatoes, herbs, and garlic. Leave the peel on potatoes for more fiber and texture. This dish can be served family-style at the table, if you prefer.

- 3 medium tomatoes, seeded and coarsely chopped
- 2 tablespoons fresh chopped basil
- 1 garlic clove, minced
- 2 tablespoons plus 1/2 cup olive oil, divided
- Sea salt and freshly ground pepper, to taste
- 3 large russet potatoes
- 4 large eggs
- 1 teaspoon fresh oregano, chopped

Put tomatoes in a food processor and puree them, skins and all.

Add the basil, garlic, 2 tablespoons olive oil, sea salt, and freshly ground pepper, and pulse to combine.

Put the mixture in a large skillet over low heat and cook, covered, for 20–25 minutes, or until the sauce has thickened and is bubbly.

Meanwhile, dice the potatoes into small cubes. Put 1/2 cup olive oil in a nonstick skillet over medium-low heat.

Fry the potatoes for 5 minutes until crisp and browned on the outside, then cover and reduce heat to low. Steam potatoes until done.

Carefully crack the eggs into the tomato sauce. Cook over low heat until the eggs are set in the sauce, about 6 minutes.

Remove the potatoes from the pan and drain them on paper towels, then place them in a bowl.

Sprinkle with sea salt and freshly ground pepper to taste and top with the oregano.

Carefully remove the eggs with a slotted spoon and place them on a plate with the potatoes. Spoon sauce over the top and serve.

Serves 2.

Honey and Avocado Smoothie

Avocados are loaded with heart-healthful monounsaturated fats and will definitely fill you up in the morning. While common in savory dishes in the Americas, in other parts of the world avocados are used in sweet drinks and desserts.

- 1 1/2 cups milk of your choice
- 1 large avocado
- 2 tablespoons honey

Add all ingredients to your blender and blend until smooth and creamy.

Serve immediately and enjoy!

Serves 2.

Peach and Walnut Breakfast Salad

Ripe fruit served in season is a hallmark of Mediterranean cuisine. This dish is light and fresh but feels just a little bit like dessert. If you prefer, substitute apples for the pears. Serve with whole-grain toast for a complete breakfast.

- 1/2 cup low-fat or nonfat cottage cheese, room temperature
- 1 ripe peach, pitted and sliced
- 1/4 cup chopped walnuts, toasted
- 1 teaspoon honey
- 1 tablespoon chopped fresh mint
- Zest of 1 lemon

Put the cottage cheese in a small bowl, and top with the peach slices and walnuts.

Drizzle with the honey, then top with the fresh mint and a pinch of lemon zest.

Serve with a spoon.

Serves 1.

Peachy Green Smoothie

You'll get many servings of fruits and vegetables in one delicious drink with this smoothie. It's perfect for days when cooking for yourself is a challenge. Don't forget to use Greek yogurt.

- 1 cup almond milk
- 3 cups kale or spinach
- 1 banana, peeled
- 1 orange, peeled
- 1 small green apple
- 1 cup frozen peaches
- 1/4 cup vanilla Greek yogurt

Put the ingredients in a blender in the order listed and blend on high until smooth.

Serve and enjoy.

Serves 2.

Savory Breakfast Oats

This savory hot cereal combines the fiber of oats with the juicy, sunny flavors common in Turkey, Greece, and Israel. Meanwhile, the herbs and pepper add a little zip.

- 1/2 cup steel-cut oats
- 1 cup water
- 1 large tomato, chopped
- 1 medium cucumber, chopped
- 1 tablespoon olive oil
- Freshly grated, low-fat Parmesan cheese
- Flat-leaf parsley or mint, chopped, for garnish
- Sea salt and freshly ground pepper, to taste

Put the oats and 1 cup of water in a medium saucepan and bring to a boil on high heat.

Stir continuously until water is absorbed, about 15 minutes.

To serve, divide the oatmeal between 2 bowls and top with the tomatoes and cucumber.

Drizzle with olive oil, then top with the Parmesan cheese and parsley or mint.

Season to taste.

Serve immediately.

Serves 2.

Scrambled Eggs with Feta and Olives

The Mediterranean is the birthplace of olives, and Spain the largest producer. Skip bland canned olives, which are cured using lye. Choose French, Italian, or Greek varieties available at olive bars, instead.

- 4 large eggs
- 1 tablespoon milk
- Sea salt, to taste
- 1 tablespoon olive oil
- 1/4 cup crumbled feta cheese
- 10 Kalamata olives, pitted and sliced
- Freshly ground pepper, to taste
- Small bunch fresh mint, chopped, for garnish

Beat the eggs with a fork or wire whisk until just combined.

Add the milk and a pinch of sea salt.

Heat a medium nonstick skillet over medium-high heat and add the olive oil.

Add the eggs and stir constantly, until they just begin to curd and firm up.

Add the feta cheese and olives, and stir until evenly combined.

Season with sea salt and freshly ground pepper to taste. Use a light hand with the salt, because the olives and feta are very salty.

Divide between 2 plates and garnish with the fresh chopped mint. Serve immediately.

Serves 2.

Spanish Tuna Tortilla with Roasted Peppers

A tortilla is a popular Spanish egg dish, similar to an omelet, but made with potatoes. While often served as a small plate or "tapa" at bars, it also makes a great breakfast dish.

- 6 large eggs
- 1/4 cup olive oil
- 2 small russet potatoes, diced
- 1 small onion, chopped
- 1 roasted red bell pepper, sliced
- 1 (7-ounce) can tuna packed in water, drained well and flaked
- 2 plum tomatoes, seeded and diced
- 1 teaspoon dried tarragon

Preheat the broiler on high.

Crack the eggs in a large bowl and whisk them together until just combined.

Heat the olive oil in a large, oven-safe, nonstick or cast-iron skillet over medium-low heat.

Add the potatoes and cook until slightly soft, about 7 minutes.

Add the onion and the peppers and cook until soft, 3–5 minutes.

Add the tuna, tomatoes, and tarragon to the skillet and stir to combine, then add the eggs.

Cook for 7–10 minutes until the eggs are bubbling from the bottom and the bottom is slightly brown.

Place the skillet into the oven on 1 of the first 2 racks, and cook until the middle is set and the top is slightly brown.

Slice into wedges and serve warm or at room temperature.

Serves 4.

Spiced Scrambled Eggs

You can enjoy whole eggs up to four times a week on the Mediterranean diet. Spicy additions like the Fresno or jalapeño peppers included here not only add flavor but can help you feel full faster. Enjoy with sliced tomatoes and whole-wheat toast.

- 2 tablespoons olive oil
- 1 small red onion, chopped
- 1 medium green pepper, cored, seeded, and finely chopped
- 1 red Fresno or jalapeño chili pepper, seeded and cut into thin strips
- 3 medium tomatoes, chopped
- Sea salt and freshly ground pepper, to taste
- 1 tablespoon ground cumin
- 1 teaspoon ground coriander
- 4 large eggs, lightly beaten

Heat the olive oil in a large, heavy skillet over medium heat.

Add the onion and cook until soft and translucent, 6–7 minutes.

Add the peppers and continue to cook until soft, another 4–5 minutes.

Add in the tomatoes and season to taste.

Stir in the cumin and coriander.

Simmer for 10 minutes over medium-low heat.

Add the eggs, stirring them into the mixture to distribute.

Cover the skillet and cook until the eggs are set but still fluffy and tender, about 5–6 minutes more.

Divide between 4 plates and serve immediately.

Serves 4

SALADS

- Arugula and Artichokes
- Asparagus Salad
- Double-Apple Spinach Salad
- Endive with Shrimp
- Four-Bean Salad
- Garden Salad with Sardine Filets
- Moroccan Tomato and Roasted Chile Salad
- Peachy Tomato Salad
- Raw Zucchini Salad
- Riviera Tuna Salad
- Tomato and Pepper Salad
- Warm Fennel, Cherry Tomato, and Spinach Salad
- Wilted Kale Salad

Arugula and Artichokes

Arugula, also known as rocket, is a dark leafy green that has a peppery bite. It's very flavorful and has plenty of vitamins A, C, and K, as well as vital phytonutrients. Make this salad with the sweetest cherry tomatoes you can find.

- 4 tablespoons olive oil
- 2 tablespoons balsamic vinegar
- 1 teaspoon Dijon mustard
- 1 clove garlic, minced
- 6 cups baby arugula leaves
- 6 oil-packed artichoke hearts, sliced
- 6 low-salt olives, pitted and chopped
- 1 cup cherry tomatoes, sliced in half
- 4 fresh basil leaves, thinly sliced

Make the dressing by whisking together the olive oil, vinegar, Dijon, and garlic until you have a smooth emulsion. Set aside.

Toss the arugula, artichokes, olives, and tomatoes together.

Drizzle the salad with the dressing, garnish with the fresh basil, and serve.

Serves 6.

Asparagus Salad

Asparagus is a spring vegetable that is as delicious raw as it is cooked. Asparagus is not only low in calories, but it is also a good source of vitamin B6, calcium, magnesium, and zinc. When choosing extra-virgin olive oil for this salad, use the highest quality available.

- 1 pound asparagus
- Sea salt and freshly ground pepper, to taste
- 4 tablespoons olive oil
- 1 tablespoon balsamic vinegar
- 1 tablespoon lemon zest

Either roast the asparagus or, with a vegetable peeler, shave it into thin strips.

Season to taste.

Toss with the olive oil and vinegar, garnish with a sprinkle of lemon zest, and serve.

Serves 4.

Double-Apple Spinach Salad

This salad is crunchy, tart, and sweet, with greens, fruits, nuts, and low-fat cheese. Its ingredients also provide a wide range of benefits—apples, walnuts, and spinach offer plenty of fiber, vitamins, minerals, and antioxidants. Serve for lunch with a whole-grain baguette, or at dinner as a first course.

- 8 cups baby spinach
- 1 medium Granny Smith apple, diced
- 1 medium red apple, diced
- 1/2 cup toasted walnuts
- 2 ounces low-fat, sharp white cheddar cheese, cubed
- 3 tablespoons olive oil
- 1 tablespoon red wine vinegar or apple cider vinegar

Toss the spinach, apples, walnuts, and cubed cheese together.

Lightly drizzle olive oil and vinegar over top and serve.

Serves 4.

Endive with Shrimp

This elegant, simple salad makes a delicious lunch entrée. The walnuts provide high levels of omega-3 fatty acids. Serve it with crusty bread and a dry white wine.

- 1/4 cup olive oil
- 1 small shallot, minced
- 1 tablespoon Dijon mustard
- Juice and zest of 1 lemon
- Sea salt and freshly ground pepper, to taste
- 2 cups salted water
- 14 shrimp, peeled and deveined
- 1 head endive
- 1/2 cup tart green apple, diced
- 2 tablespoons toasted walnuts

For the vinaigrette, whisk together the first five ingredients in a small bowl until creamy and emulsified.

Refrigerate for at least 2 hours for best flavor.

In a small pan, boil salted water. Add the shrimp and cook 1–2 minutes, or until the shrimp turns pink. Drain and cool under cold water.

To assemble the salad, wash and break the endive. Place on serving plates and top with the shrimp, green apple, and toasted walnuts.

Drizzle with the vinaigrette before serving.

Serves 4.

Four-Bean Salad

Beans are a staple in many parts of the Mediterranean. High in fiber, beans are also versatile and can be eaten hot or cold, in salads or soups. Use dried beans for the best flavor, but keep canned beans on hand as a convenient option.

- 1/2 cup white beans, cooked
- 1/2 cup black-eyed peas, cooked
- 1/2 cup fava beans, cooked
- 1/2 cup lima beans, cooked
- 1 red bell pepper, diced
- 1 small bunch flat-leaf parsley, chopped
- 2 tablespoons olive oil
- 1 teaspoon ground cumin
- Juice of 1 lemon
- Sea salt and freshly ground pepper, to taste

You can cook the beans a day or two in advance to speed up the preparation of this dish.

Combine all ingredients in a large bowl and mix well.

Season to taste.

Allow to sit for 30 minutes, so the flavors can come together before serving.

Serves 4.

Garden Salad with Sardine Filets

This tasty salad combines traditional Mediterranean ingredients. Sardines are a superfood, containing vitamins B3, B12, and D, as well as tryptophan, selenium, omega-3 fats, protein, phosphorus, and calcium. You can serve this salad as a side dish, or a as a main dish with whole-wheat bread or breadsticks.

- 1/2 cup olive oil
- Juice of 1 medium lemon
- 1 teaspoon Dijon mustard
- Sea salt and freshly ground pepper, to taste
- 4 medium tomatoes, diced
- 1 large cucumber, peeled and diced
- 1 pound arugula, trimmed and chopped
- 1 small red onion, thinly sliced
- 1 small bunch flat-leaf parsley, chopped
- 4 whole sardine filets packed in olive oil, drained and chopped

For the dressing, whisk together the olive oil, lemon juice, and mustard, and season with sea salt and pepper. Set aside.

In a large bowl, combine all the vegetables with the parsley, and toss.

Add the sardine filets on top of the salad.

Drizzle the dressing over the salad just before serving.

Serves 6.

Moroccan Tomato and Roasted Chile Salad

The Mediterranean diet is based on plenty of vegetables, and this is great way to get them in one satisfying dish. Serve with grilled chicken or kebabs to make this a main dish.

- 2 large green bell peppers
- 1 hot red chili Fresno or jalapeño pepper
- 4 large tomatoes, peeled, seeded, and diced
- 1 large cucumber, peeled and diced
- 1 small bunch flat-leaf parsley, chopped
- 4 tablespoons olive oil
- 1 teaspoon ground cumin
- Juice of 1 lemon
- Sea salt and freshly ground pepper, to taste

Preheat broiler on high. Broil all of the peppers and chilies until the skin blackens and blisters.

Place the peppers and chilies in a paper bag. Seal and set aside to cool.

Combine the rest of the ingredients in a medium bowl and mix well.

Take peppers and chilies out from the bag and remove the skins. Seed and chop the peppers and add them to the salad.

Season with sea salt and freshly ground pepper.

Toss to combine and let sit for 15–20 minutes before serving.

Serves 6.

Peachy Tomato Salad

A variety of salads help provide the fruits and vegetables that make up the foundation of the Mediterranean diet. Make this super-easy side dish in the summer when both tomatoes and peaches are at their best. The sweet and savory flavors combined in this fruit salad pair best with grilled fare.

- 2 ripe peaches, pitted and sliced into wedges
- 2 ripe tomatoes, cut into wedges
- 1/2 red onion, thinly sliced
- Sea salt and freshly ground pepper, to taste
- 3 tablespoons olive oil
- 1 tablespoon lemon juice

Toss the peaches, tomatoes, and red onion in a large bowl.

Season to taste.

Add the olive oil and lemon juice, and gently toss.

Serve at room temperature.

Serves 2.

Raw Zucchini Salad

This light and robust salad makes an excellent starter. Zucchini and tomatoes are both summer vegetables that provide good nutrition as well as hydration. The key to creating this dish is to slice the zucchini paper-thin or shred into long, thin slices with a cheese grater.

- 1 medium zucchini, shredded or sliced paper thin
- 6 cherry tomatoes, halved
- 3 tablespoons olive oil
- Juice of 1 lemon
- Sea salt and freshly ground pepper, to taste
- 3–4 basil leaves, thinly sliced
- 2 tablespoons freshly grated, low-fat Parmesan cheese

Layer the zucchini slices on 2 plates in even layers.

Top with the tomatoes.

Drizzle with the olive oil and lemon juice.

Season to taste.

Top with the basil and sprinkle with cheese before serving.

Serves 2.

Riviera Tuna Salad

Humble canned tuna becomes something special in this healthful, main-dish salad, while garbanzo beans add fiber and protein.

- 1/4 cup olive oil
- 1/4 cup balsamic vinegar
- 1/2 teaspoon minced garlic
- 1/4 teaspoon dried oregano
- Sea salt and freshly ground pepper, to taste
- 2 tablespoons capers, drained
- 4–6 cups baby greens
- 1 (6-ounce) can solid white albacore tuna, drained
- 1 cup canned garbanzo beans, rinsed and drained
- 1/4 cup low-salt olives, pitted and quartered
- 2 Roma tomatoes, chopped

To make the vinaigrette, whisk together the olive oil, balsamic vinegar, garlic, oregano, sea salt, and pepper until emulsified.

Stir in the capers. Refrigerate for up to 6 hours before serving.

Place the baby greens in a salad bowl or on individual plates, and top with the tuna, beans, olives, and tomatoes.

Drizzle the vinaigrette over all, and serve immediately.

Serves 4.

Tomato and Pepper Salad

Tomatoes are a staple in Spain, as they are in Italy and the south of France. Yellow peppers have more nutrients than green peppers and a milder, sweeter flavor. Enjoy this salad with any grilled lean meat or poultry.

- 3 large yellow peppers
- 1/4 cup olive oil
- 1 small bunch fresh basil leaves
- 2 cloves garlic, minced
- 4 large tomatoes, seeded and diced
- Sea salt and freshly ground pepper, to taste

Preheat broiler to high heat and broil the peppers until blackened on all sides.

Remove from heat and place in a paper bag. Seal and allow peppers to cool.

Once cooled, peel the skins off the peppers, then seed and chop them.

Add half of the peppers to a food processor along with the olive oil, basil, and garlic, and pulse several times to make the dressing.

Combine the rest of the peppers with the tomatoes and toss with the dressing.

Season the salad with sea salt and freshly ground pepper.

Allow salad to come to room temperature before serving.

Serves 6.

Warm Fennel, Cherry Tomato, and Spinach Salad

Slightly wilted spinach contrasts nicely with the crunchy fennel in this salad that can serve as a side dish or even a light lunch.

- 4 tablespoons chicken broth
- 4 cups baby spinach leaves
- 10 cherry tomatoes, halved
- Sea salt and freshly ground pepper, to taste
- 1 fennel bulb, sliced
- 1/4 cup olive oil
- Juice of 2 lemons

In a large sauté pan, heat the chicken broth over medium heat. Add the spinach and tomatoes and cook until spinach is wilted. Season with sea salt and freshly ground pepper to taste.

Remove from heat and toss fennel slices in with the spinach and tomatoes. Let the fennel warm in the pan, then transfer to a large bowl.

Drizzle with the olive oil and lemon juice, and serve immediately.

Serves 2.

Wilted Kale Salad

Kale can be eaten raw, cooked, or gently sautéed—as it is in this recipe—with a little garlic, olive oil, and cherry tomatoes. A nutrient powerhouse, kale is extremely high in vitamins A, C, and K. Use a lid to help wilt the kale and keep it in the pan.

- 2 heads kale
- 1+ tablespoon olive oil
- 2 cloves garlic, minced
- 1 cup cherry tomatoes, sliced
- Sea salt and freshly ground pepper, to taste
- Juice of 1 lemon

Rinse and dry kale.

Tear the kale into bite-sized pieces.

Heat 1 tablespoon of the olive oil in a large skillet, and add the garlic.

Cook for 1 minute and then add the kale.

Cook just until wilted, then add the tomatoes.

Cook until tomatoes are softened, then remove from heat.

Place tomatoes and kale in a bowl, and season with sea salt and freshly ground pepper.

Drizzle with remaining olive oil and lemon juice, serve, and enjoy.

Serves 4.

SIDES AND SNACKS

- Anchovy and Red Pepper Antipasto
- Baked Kale Chips
- Chili Shrimp
- Classic Hummus
- Dolmades
- Italian Breaded Shrimp Stuffed with Couscous
- Marinated Olives and Mushrooms
- Mini Lettuce Wraps
- Mini Moroccan Pumpkin Cakes
- Roasted Eggplant Dip with Spicy Yogurt Sauce and Homemade Pita Chips
- Salted Almonds
- Sardines in Tomato Sauce
- Toasted Pita Wedges

Anchovy and Red Pepper Antipasto

"Antipasto" literally means "before the meal." Strong savory flavors are more satisfying than bland crackers and cheese, so you may find yourself eating less. Serve with whole-grain bread sticks or bread toasted with olive oil.

- 4 red peppers
- 6 ounces anchovies in oil, chopped
- 1 small shallot
- 2 tablespoons capers, rinsed and drained
- 1 cup Kalamata olives, pitted
- 1/2 cup olive oil
- Sea salt and freshly ground pepper, to taste

Heat the grill to medium-high heat.

Place the red peppers on the grill and cook, turning frequently, until the skins are charred.

Place the peppers in a paper bag and allow them to rest for 10 minutes.

Once the peppers have cooled, peel the skins off under cold water, then pat dry with paper towels.

Combine the anchovies, shallot, capers, olives, and olive oil in a large bowl.

Cut the peppers into chunks and toss with the anchovy mixture. Season to taste.

Serve with crusty bread or water crackers.

Serves 4.

Baked Kale Chips

If you're looking for a crunchy snack to munch on instead of potato chips, you'll love these kale chips. Kale is extremely low in calories and is one of the most nutrient-dense foods on the planet. Crunchy and flavorful, these will help you easily meet the daily requirement of vegetables.

- 2 heads curly leaf kale
- 2 tablespoons olive oil
- Sea salt, to taste

Tear the kale into bite-sized pieces.

Toss with the olive oil, and lay on a baking sheet in a single layer.

Sprinkle with a pinch of sea salt.

Bake for 10–15 minutes until crispy.

Serve or store in an airtight container.

Makes about 4 cups chips.

Chili Shrimp

This tasty and spicy side dish is great for potlucks and other fun occasions.

- 1/2 cup olive oil
- 5 cloves garlic, minced
- 1 teaspoon red pepper flakes
- 24 large shrimp, peeled and deveined
- Juice and zest from 1 lemon
- Sea salt and freshly ground pepper, to taste

Heat the olive oil in a large skillet over medium-high heat.

Add the garlic and red pepper flakes, and cook for 1 minute.

Add the shrimp and cook an additional 3 minutes, stirring frequently.

Remove from the pan, and sprinkle with lemon juice, sea salt, and pepper.

Serves 6.

Classic Hummus

Hummus is a creamy and delicious dip that can be served as an appetizer, at a party, or just as a snack. Try using hummus in place of mayonnaise on sandwiches.

- 3 cups cooked chickpeas, slightly warmed
- 1/4 cup olive oil
- Juice of 2 lemons
- 2–3 cloves garlic
- 3/4 cup tahini
- Sea salt and freshly ground pepper, to taste
- 1/2 cup pine nuts, toasted (optional)
- 1/4 cup flat-leaf parsley, chopped

Add the chickpeas, olive oil, lemon juice, and garlic to a food processor, and puree until smooth.

Add the tahini and continue to blend until creamy.

If too thick, a bit of water can be used to thin it out.

Season with sea salt and freshly ground pepper to taste.

Add the pine nuts if desired, and garnish with chopped parsley.

Serve with fresh veggies or whole-wheat pita wedges.

Serves 6–8.

Dolmades

Dolmades are stuffed grape leaves, a popular appetizer in Greece, where they are usually served with tzatziki, a cucumber yogurt sauce. This complex vegetarian version features rice, herbs, buttery pine nuts, sweet raisins, and tangy lemon.

- 1 tablespoon olive oil
- 3 shallots, chopped
- 2 cloves garlic, minced
- 3/4 cup short-grain rice
- 1/4 cup gold raisins
- 1/4 cup pine nuts, toasted
- Juice of 1 lemon
- Sea salt and freshly ground pepper, to taste
- 2/3 cup water
- 4 green onions, chopped
- 1 small bunch mint leaves, finely chopped
- 1 small bunch flat-leaf parsley, chopped
- 20 preserved grape leaves

Heat the olive oil in large skillet over medium heat.

Add the shallots and garlic, and sauté for 5 minutes.

Add the rice, golden raisins, pine nuts, and lemon juice. Season with sea salt and freshly ground pepper.

Add 2/3 cup water, bring to a boil, and cover. Reduce heat and simmer for 20 minutes.

Turn off heat and allow rice to cool.

Add the green onions and herbs to the rice filling and mix well.

Rinse the grape leaves in water and stuff each leaf with about 1 tablespoon of the filling.

Roll tightly and place each in a steamer, seam side down.

Steam for about 10 minutes, until leaves are tender.

Serve warm.

Makes 20.

Italian Breaded Shrimp Stuffed with Couscous

Couscous and shrimp have one thing in common (besides being delicious): they are both super fast to cook. Sundried tomatoes and pesto add Italian flavor to this festive dish. Use the largest shrimp you can find to make the stuffing easy.

- 1 cup vegetable stock
- 1/2 cup whole-wheat couscous
- 12 extra-large shrimp, peeled and deveined
- 1 egg, beaten
- 1/4 cup Italian-seasoned breadcrumbs
- 1 tablespoon olive oil
- 2 sundried tomatoes, finely chopped
- 1 tablespoon prepared pesto sauce
- Sea salt and freshly ground pepper, to taste

Bring stock to a boil and add the couscous.

Cover and remove from heat. Set aside for about 5 minutes.

Coat the shrimp with the egg and dredge in the breadcrumbs.

In a large sauté pan, heat the olive oil and add the shrimp, cooking until just brown and crispy on all sides.

Remove the lid from the couscous, then stir in the sundried tomatoes and pesto.

Season with sea salt and freshly ground pepper.

To stuff the shrimp, slice the front of the shrimp open and spoon the couscous mixture inside.

Serve with leftover couscous on the side.

Serves 2.

Marinated Olives and Mushrooms

Tangy and salty olives combine with mild button mushrooms to make a marinated treat. These savory morsels are easy to prepare and are especially good to serve at a party. Store in the refrigerator for up to three days, but serve at room temperature.

- 1 pound white button mushrooms
- 1 pound mixed, high-quality olives
- 2 tablespoons fresh thyme leaves
- 1 tablespoon white wine vinegar
- 1/2 tablespoon crushed fennel seeds
- Pinch chili flakes
- Olive oil, to cover
- Sea salt and freshly ground pepper, to taste

Clean and rinse mushrooms under cold water and pat dry.

Combine all ingredients in a glass jar or other airtight container. Cover with olive oil and season with sea salt and freshly ground pepper.

Shake to distribute the ingredients.

Allow to marinate for at least 1 hour.

Serve at room temperature.

Serves 8.

Mini Lettuce Wraps

Like a Greek salad wrapped in lettuce, this bite-sized appetizer is easy to assemble. Swap out the tomatoes, cucumbers, and red onion for any vegetables you like. Serve the wraps on their own or as part of a larger selection of appetizers.

- 1 tomato, diced
- 1 cucumber, diced
- 1 red onion, sliced
- 1 ounce low-fat feta cheese, crumbled
- Juice of 1 lemon
- 1 tablespoon olive oil
- Sea salt and freshly ground pepper, to taste
- 12 small, intact iceberg lettuce leaves

Combine the tomato, cucumber, onion, and feta in a bowl with the lemon juice and olive oil.

Season with sea salt and freshly ground pepper.

Without tearing the leaves, gently fill each leaf with a tablespoon of the veggie mixture.

Roll them as tightly as you can, and lay them seam-side-down on a serving platter.

Makes about 1 dozen wraps.

Mini Moroccan Pumpkin Cakes

Pumpkin is served in savory Moroccan tagines. These spicy and savory pan-fried cakes of pumpkin, rice, and walnuts can also be served as a side dish, and are a tasty way to get your daily requirement of nuts.

- 2 cups cooked brown rice
- 1 cup pumpkin puree
- 1/2 cup finely chopped walnuts
- 3 tablespoons olive oil, divided
- 1/2 medium onion, diced
- 1/2 red bell pepper, diced
- 1 teaspoon ground cumin
- Sea salt and freshly ground pepper, to taste
- 1 teaspoon hot paprika or a pinch of cayenne

Combine the rice, pumpkin, and walnuts in a large bowl; set aside.

In a medium skillet, heat the olive oil over medium heat, add the onion and bell pepper, and cook until soft, about 5 minutes.

Add the cumin to the onions and bell peppers.

Add onion mixture to the rice mixture.

Mix thoroughly and season with sea salt, freshly ground pepper, and paprika or cayenne.

In a large skillet, heat 2 tablespoons of olive oil over medium heat.

Form the rice mixture into 1-inch patties and add them to the skillet. Cook until both sides are browned and crispy.

Serve with Greek yogurt or tzatziki on the side.

Serves 6.

Roasted Eggplant Dip with Spicy Yogurt Sauce and Homemade Pita Chips

Roasting eggplant softens it and adds a smoky flavor. This dip is reminiscent of Lebanese baba ghanoush, and the yogurt dip is much like Greek tzatziki. For added nutrition, include raw vegetables with the pita chips for dipping.

For the eggplant dip:

- 2 large eggplants
- Pinch of sea salt
- Juice of 2 lemons
- 2 bell peppers, diced
- 2 roasted red peppers, diced
- 2 cups diced tomatoes
- 20 yellow or red cherry tomatoes
- 5 cloves garlic, minced
- 1/2 cup chopped flat-leaf parsley
- 1/4 cup chives, chopped
- 3 basil leaves, slivered
- 1 tablespoon olive oil
- Sea salt and freshly ground pepper, to taste

For the yogurt sauce:

- 1 cup Greek yogurt
- 1/2 cucumber, grated
- 2 tablespoons fresh dill, chopped
- 1 clove garlic, minced
- 1 jalapeño, chopped
- Sea salt and freshly ground pepper, to taste

For the pita chips:

- 4 whole-wheat pitas, each cut into 12 triangles
- 2 tablespoons olive oil
- 1 teaspoon sesame seeds
- Sea salt and freshly ground pepper, to taste

Make the eggplant dip:

Preheat oven to 450 degrees.

Salt both sides of the sliced eggplant, and let sit for 20 minutes to draw out the bitter juices. Rinse the eggplant and pat dry with a paper towel.

Roast eggplants until they fall, about 35 minutes.

Cool and cut open, scooping out the flesh. Throw away skins.

Drizzle eggplant with lemon juice and put into a strainer, then squeeze out moisture.

Chop and mix with peppers, tomato, garlic, herbs, and olive oil.

Season with sea salt and freshly ground pepper.

Make the yogurt sauce:
Mix yogurt, cucumber, dill, garlic, and jalapeño. Season with sea salt and freshly ground pepper.

Make the pita chips:
Reduce oven to 350 degrees.

Lay wedges on baking sheet, then drizzle with olive oil, sprinkle with sesame seeds, sea salt, and freshly ground pepper.

Bake for 10–15 minutes until crisp.

Serve the pita chips with the yogurt sauce and roasted eggplant.

Serves 8.

Salted Almonds

These almonds are easy to prepare and make a great snack to serve at a party. High in healthful fats, almonds provide manganese, vitamin E, magnesium, and more. They are often served alongside tapas in Spain.

- 1 cup raw almonds
- 1 egg white, beaten
- 1/2 teaspoon coarse sea salt

Preheat oven to 350 degrees.

Spread the almonds in an even layer on a baking sheet.

Bake for 20 minutes until lightly browned and fragrant.

Coat the almonds with the egg white and sprinkle with the salt.

Put back in the oven for about 5 minutes until they have dried.

Cool completely before serving.

Makes 1 cup.

Sardines in Tomato Sauce

Sardines are plentiful, cheap, and sustainable. Best of all, they're full of healthful omega-3 fatty acids. They're easy to prepare, since the spine lifts out easily and takes all the bones with it.

- 2 pounds fresh sardines
- 3 tablespoons olive oil, divided
- 1 small onion, sliced thinly
- 4 Roma tomatoes, peeled and chopped
- Zest of 1 orange
- Sea salt and freshly ground pepper, to taste
- 2 tablespoons whole-wheat breadcrumbs
- 1/2 cup white wine

Preheat the oven to 425 degrees.

Clean the sardines under running water. Slit the belly, remove the spine, and butterfly the fish.

Brush a little olive oil in a baking dish.

Heat the remaining olive oil in a large skillet.

Add the onion, tomatoes, orange zest, sea salt, and freshly ground pepper, and simmer for 20 minutes, or until the mixture thickens and softens.

Place half the sauce in the bottom of the casserole dish.

Set the fish on top, and spread the remaining sauce over the fish.

Top with the breadcrumbs and white wine, and bake for 20 minutes.

Serve immediately.

Serves 4.

Toasted Pita Wedges

A sandwich-style pocket bread, pita bread is a staple all over the Mediterranean region. It can be served alongside salads and soups, and with dips and spreads. You can buy pita chips, but these wedges are easy to prepare and much healthier since you control the amount of oil.

- 4 whole-wheat pita rounds
- 1 tablespoon olive oil
- 1 teaspoon garlic powder
- 1/4 teaspoon paprika
- Sea salt and freshly ground pepper, to taste

Preheat oven to 400 degrees.

Cut the pita rounds into 8 wedges each, and lay on a parchment-lined baking sheet in an even layer.

Drizzle with olive oil, and sprinkle with garlic powder and paprika.

Season with sea salt and freshly ground pepper.

Bake for 10–12 minutes, until wedges are lightly browned and crisp.

Allow to cool completely before serving for crisper wedges.

Makes 32 wedges.

SOUPS

- Cold Cucumber Soup
- Cream of Mushroom Soup with Red Wine
- Farro Bean Soup
- Hazelnut Soup
- Lentil Soup with Spinach
- Roasted Eggplant Soup
- Roasted Red Pepper and Feta Soup
- Shrimp Soup with Leeks and Fennel
- Spinach and Brown Rice Soup
- Tomato Soup
- Turkish Lentil Soup
- White Bean, Cherry Tomato, and Kale Soup
- Zuppa di Fagioli

Cold Cucumber Soup

Nothing's more refreshing on a hot day than this classic Greek soup. Serve it with pita bread or a salad for a light lunch or dinner. Nonfat yogurt is fine in this soup, or you can use strained conventional yogurt instead of Greek yogurt.

- 2 seedless cucumbers, peeled and cut into chunks
- 2 cups plain Greek yogurt
- 1/2 cup mint, finely chopped
- 2 garlic cloves, minced
- 2 cups chicken broth or vegetable stock
- 3 teaspoons fresh dill
- 1 tablespoon tomato paste
- Sea salt and freshly ground pepper, to taste

Puree the cucumber, yogurt, mint, and garlic in a food processor or blender.

Add the chicken broth, dill, tomato paste, sea salt, and pepper, and blend completely.

Refrigerate for at least 2 hours before serving.

Serves 4.

Cream of Mushroom Soup with Red Wine

The classic flavors of Italy—red wine and mushrooms—are combined in this rich and creamy soup. Mushrooms are a good source of vitamins B2, B3, and B5, as well as selenium. Substitute crimini or oyster mushrooms for the button mushrooms, if you prefer.

- 2 ounces dried porcini
- 2 ounces dried morels
- 8 ounces portobello mushrooms, chopped
- 8 ounces button mushrooms, chopped
- 1 tablespoon olive oil
- 1 teaspoon butter
- 3 shallots, finely chopped
- 2 cloves garlic, minced
- 1 teaspoon finely chopped fresh thyme
- Sea salt and freshly ground pepper, to taste
- 4 cups mushroom stock or chicken broth
- 1/3 cup dry red wine or sherry
- 1/2 cup heavy cream
- 1 small bunch flat-leaf parsley, chopped

Reconstitute the dried mushrooms by pouring enough warm water over them to cover. Allow the mushrooms to sit for 30 minutes and drain.

In a large Dutch oven or stockpot, heat the olive oil and butter over medium-high heat.

Add the mushrooms and shallots, and cook for 10 minutes, until mushrooms are softened.

Add the garlic and cook for 1 more minute.

Add the thyme, and season with sea salt and freshly ground pepper to taste.

Add the broth and wine and bring to a boil on high heat. Reduce heat to low and simmer for 20 minutes.

Remove half of the soup, puree in a food processor or blender, then add it back to the pan. This will thicken the soup while still leaving some of the mushrooms intact for textural contrast.

Stir in the cream and warm through.

Pour into bowls, garnish with the chopped parsley, and serve.

Serves 6.

Farro Bean Soup

This soup is easy and inexpensive to make, highly nutritious, and simply comforting. Find the traditional Italian grain farro or emmer wheat at a health food store or warehouse store if your grocer doesn't carry it.

- 2 tablespoons olive oil
- 1 medium onion, diced
- 1 celery stalk, diced
- 2 garlic cloves, minced
- 8 cups chicken broth or water
- 1 cup white beans, soaked overnight, rinsed, and drained
- 1 (14-ounce) can diced tomatoes, with juice
- 1 cup farro
- 1/2 teaspoon thyme
- 1/2 teaspoon freshly ground pepper
- 2 bay leaves
- Sea salt and freshly ground pepper, to taste

Heat the olive oil in a large stockpot on medium-high heat.

Sauté the onion, celery, and garlic cloves just until tender.

Add the broth or water, beans, tomatoes, farro, and seasonings, and bring to a simmer.

Cover and cook for 2 hours, or until the beans and farro are tender.

Season with sea salt and freshly ground pepper to taste.

Serves 8.

Hazelnut Soup

Sweet, creamy, and delicious, this light soup from Spain makes an excellent starter course. Hazelnuts are a great source of protein, folate, vitamins B6 and E, and amino acid arginine. Serve it with a green salad and sliced green apples.

- 4 ounces hazelnuts
- 4 tablespoons olive oil
- 4 leeks, white parts only, sliced
- 1/2 onion, diced
- 4 cups chicken stock, divided
- 1/4 cup heavy cream
- 2 tablespoons chopped chives

Preheat the oven to 350 degrees.

Spread the hazelnuts on a baking sheet and toast for 5 minutes.

Cool nuts in the refrigerator and process 3 ounces of the nuts in a food processor until fine. Reserve the remaining nuts for a garnish.

Heat the olive oil in a medium saucepan.

Add the leeks and onion, and sauté over low heat until tender.

Add 1/2 cup chicken stock, then puree the mixture in a blender until smooth.

Return the chicken stock mixture to the saucepan. Add the remaining chicken stock and simmer for 10 minutes.

Stir in the heavy cream until combined.

Pour into bowls and garnish with the unprocessed hazelnuts and chives.

Serves 4.

Lentil Soup with Spinach

Lentils are a staple of the Mediterranean diet. They are similar to beans as far as flavor and nutrients go, but they have one distinct advantage when it comes to preparation: they cook much faster. Though rich and creamy, they are also very low in calories. Pair these with a light red wine, such as Pinot Noir.

- 1 teaspoon olive oil
- 1 cup onion, chopped
- 1 1/2 cups lentils
- 1 tablespoon curry powder
- 6 cups water
- 12 ounces spinach

Heat the olive oil and sauté the onion.

Add the lentils and curry powder and stir.

Add the water and cook until lentils are tender, about 15–20 minutes.

Add the spinach and stir until wilted.

Serve with toasted whole-wheat bread and a green salad.

Serves 6.

Roasted Eggplant Soup

Fresh herbs add flavor to this soup as well as powerful nutrients and antioxidants. This makes an excellent meal on its own if served with bread, but it can also be served as a first course.

- 3 large eggplants, sliced lengthwise
- Pinch sea salt
- 2 tablespoons olive oil
- 1 medium red onion, chopped
- 2 tablespoons garlic, minced
- 1 teaspoon dried thyme
- Sea salt and freshly ground pepper, to taste
- 2 large ripe tomatoes, halved
- 5 cups chicken broth
- 1/4 cup low-fat cream
- Small bunch fresh mint, chopped

Preheat oven to 400 degrees.

Salt both sides of the sliced eggplant, and let sit for 20 minutes to draw out the bitter juices. Rinse the eggplant and pat dry with a paper towel.

Place the eggplants on a sheet pan, and put them in the oven.

Roast for 45 minutes. Remove from oven and allow to cool. When cool, remove all of the insides, discarding the skins.

Heat the olive oil in a large skillet over medium heat.

Add the onions and garlic, and cook for 5 minutes until soft and translucent.

Add the thyme and season with sea salt and freshly ground pepper.

Put the eggplant, tomatoes, and onion in a food processor, and process until smooth.

Put the chicken broth in a pot, and bring to a boil. Reduce heat to a simmer, and add the eggplant mixture.

Stir until well combined, and fold in the cream.

Season to taste.

Serve the soup garnished with the fresh mint.

Serves 8.

Roasted Red Pepper and Feta Soup

Roasted red peppers make a sweet soup. When you add the salty feta, you get a savory combination that will make you think of Greece. Serve with a pita sandwich to complete the meal.

- 10 red peppers, peeled, roasted, seeded, and chopped
- 2 red chili peppers, peeled, roasted, and seeded
- 2 tablespoons olive oil
- 1 medium red onion, chopped
- 4 garlic cloves, minced
- 2 teaspoons finely chopped fresh oregano
- 6 cups chicken broth
- Sea salt and freshly ground pepper, to taste
- 1/4 cup cream
- Juice of 1 lemon
- 6 tablespoons crumbled Greek feta

Put all of the roasted peppers in a food processor and process until smooth.

Heat the olive oil in a large Dutch oven on medium-high heat and add the onion and garlic. Cook until soft and translucent, about 5 minutes.

Add the pepper mixture and oregano, followed by the broth.

Bring to a boil on high heat and season with sea salt and freshly ground pepper to taste.

Reduce heat to low and simmer for 15 minutes.

Stir in the cream and lemon juice.

Pour into bowls, top with the crumbled feta, and serve immediately.

Serves 6.

Shrimp Soup with Leeks and Fennel

The Provençal flavors of leeks, fennel, garlic, and shrimp are featured in this elegant soup. Soup like this is low in calories yet filling, and provides several servings of vegetables. You can substitute scallops for the shrimp, if you prefer.

- 2 tablespoons olive oil
- 3 stalks celery, chopped
- 1 leek, both whites and light green parts, sliced
- 1 medium fennel bulb, chopped
- 1 clove garlic, minced
- Sea salt and freshly ground pepper, to taste
- 1 tablespoon fennel seeds
- 4 cups vegetable or chicken broth
- 1 pound medium shrimp, peeled and deveined
- 2 tablespoons light cream
- Juice of 1 lemon

Heat the oil in a large Dutch oven over medium heat.

Add the celery, leek, and fennel, and cook for about 15 minutes, until vegetables are browned and very soft.

Add the garlic and season with sea salt and freshly ground pepper to taste.

Add the fennel seed and stir.

Add the broth and bring to a boil, then reduce to a simmer and cook about 20 more minutes.

Add the shrimp to the soup and cook until just pink, about 3 minutes.

Add the cream and lemon juice, and serve immediately.

Serves 6.

Spinach and Brown Rice Soup

This recipe calls for a lot of spinach; however, cooking the spinach reduces its volume significantly.

- 1 tablespoon olive oil
- 1 large onion, chopped
- 2 cloves garlic, minced
- 3 pounds spinach leaves, stems removed and leaves chopped
- 8 cups chicken broth
- 1/2 cup long-grain brown rice
- Sea salt and freshly ground pepper, to taste

Heat the olive oil in a large Dutch oven over medium heat, and add the onion and garlic.

Cook until the onions are soft and translucent, about 5 minutes.

Add the spinach and stir.

Cover the pot and cook the spinach until wilted, about 3 more minutes.

Using a slotted spoon, remove the spinach and onions from the pot, leaving the liquid.

Put the spinach mixture in a food processor or blender, and process until smooth, then return to the pot.

Add the chicken broth and bring to a boil.

Add the rice, reduce heat, and simmer until rice is cooked, about 45 minutes.

Season to taste.

Serve hot.

Serves 6.

Tomato Soup

This version of tomato soup is subtly flavored with the classic spices of Morocco—paprika, ginger, cumin, and cinnamon. In terms of nutrients, cooked tomatoes are a great source of lycopene.

- 2 tablespoons olive oil
- 1 large onion, coarsely chopped
- 8 large tomatoes, seeded and coarsely chopped
- 1 teaspoon paprika
- 1 teaspoon fresh ginger, finely chopped
- 1 teaspoon ground cumin
- 2 cups chicken broth
- 1 cinnamon stick
- 1 teaspoon honey
- Sea salt and freshly ground pepper, to taste
- Juice of 1 lemon
- 1 small bunch flat-leaf parsley, chopped
- 2 tablespoons chopped cilantro

Heat a large Dutch oven over medium-high heat.

Add the olive oil and onion, and cook until soft and translucent.

Add the tomatoes and the seasonings and stir.

Pour in the chicken broth, and add the cinnamon stick and honey.

Simmer for 15 minutes, and puree the soup in a food processor or blender (remove the cinnamon stick for this step and return it when done).

Pour back into the pot, and season with sea salt and freshly ground pepper to taste.

Stir in the lemon juice and serve garnished with the cilantro and parsley.

Serves 6.

Turkish Lentil Soup

Lentil soup is one of the most inexpensive, nutritious foods you can make. If you can't find green lentils, substitute brown. This Turkish-inspired recipe is vegetarian, but feel free to add shredded ham or chicken for a more robust dish.

- 2 tablespoons olive oil
- 1 small onion, diced
- 2 tablespoons flour
- 4 cups water or chicken stock
- 1 1/2 cups green lentils
- 1 carrot, peeled and diced
- 1/2 teaspoon dried thyme
- 1 teaspoon sea salt
- 1/2 teaspoon freshly ground pepper

Heat the olive oil in a large stockpot on medium-high heat.

Sauté the onions just until tender and translucent.

Whisk in the flour, stirring for 30 seconds until thickened into a paste.

Slowly, whisk in the water or chicken stock 1/4 cup at a time, and bring to a boil, stirring frequently.

Add the lentils, carrot, and seasonings. Cover and simmer for 1 hour, or until lentils are tender.

Serves 6.

White Bean, Cherry Tomato, and Kale Soup

White beans and kale are typical of Tuscany. This soup is as inexpensive as it is filling and nutritious. If you want to make this completely vegetarian, substitute vegetable stock.

- 2 tablespoons olive oil
- 1 small onion, chopped
- 2 cloves garlic, minced
- 1 bunch kale, torn into bite-size pieces
- 6 cups chicken or vegetable broth
- 2 pints cherry tomatoes, halved
- 2 cans white beans of your choice, drained and rinsed
- Sea salt and freshly ground pepper, to taste
- Freshly grated, low-fat Parmesan cheese

Heat the olive oil in a large soup pot or Dutch oven over medium heat.

Add the onions and cook for 5 minutes, or until soft and translucent.

Add the garlic and cook for 1 more minute.

Add the kale and stir until well coated with the olive oil.

Add the broth and bring to boil on high heat.

Reduce heat to low, and simmer for 15 minutes, until kale is softened.

Add the tomatoes and beans, and simmer for 5 more minutes.

Season with sea salt and freshly ground pepper to taste.

To serve, ladle into bowls, and sprinkle with freshly grated, low-fat Parmesan cheese.

Serves 4.

Zuppa di Fagioli

Traditionally, this Tuscan soup is made with cannellini beans or cranberry beans. Nutritionally, beans are great for lowering cholesterol. If you can't find cannellini beans, use navy beans, white beans, or even chickpeas.

- 2 tablespoons olive oil
- 3 carrots, peeled and diced
- 1 onion, chopped
- 2 cloves garlic, chopped
- 8 cups water or chicken broth
- 2 cups dried beans, soaked overnight, rinsed, and drained
- 1 teaspoon fresh thyme
- 1 bay leaf
- Sea salt and freshly ground pepper, to taste
- 8 slices whole-wheat bread
- Freshly grated, low-fat Parmesan cheese

Heat the olive oil in a large stockpot on medium heat.

Add the carrots and onion, and sauté until the onions are translucent.

Add the garlic and sauté 1 minute more.

Add the water or chicken broth, the beans, and the seasonings, and cover.

Bring to a boil on high heat, then reduce heat and simmer for 2 hours, or until the beans are tender.

Season to taste, and top with a slice of toasted whole-wheat bread and grated Parmesan cheese.

Serves 8.

6

SANDWICHES AND WRAPS

- Avocado and Asparagus Wraps
- Beef Gyros
- Cucumber Basil Sandwiches
- Falafel
- Greek Salad Pita
- Grilled Chicken Salad Pita
- Grilled Eggplant and Feta Sandwiches
- Mediterranean Tuna Salad Sandwiches
- Open-Faced Eggplant Parmesan Sandwich
- Open-Faced Grilled Caesar Salad Sandwiches
- Slow-Roasted Tomato and Basil Panini
- Spinach and Mushroom Pita

Avocado and Asparagus Wraps

Avocados are not just for guacamole—they provide a great addition to the Mediterranean diet because of their healthful fats. Use mashed avocados in place of mayonnaise in salads, sandwiches, and wraps. This wrap is served warm, and can also work as a light meal or snack.

- 12 spears asparagus
- 1 ripe avocado, mashed slightly
- Juice of 1 lime
- 2 cloves garlic, minced
- 2 cups brown rice, cooked and chilled
- 3 tablespoons Greek yogurt
- Sea salt and freshly ground pepper, to taste
- 3 (8-inch) whole-grain tortillas
- 1/2 cup cilantro, diced
- 2 tablespoons red onion, diced

Steam asparagus in microwave or stove top steamer until tender.

Mash the avocado, lime juice, and garlic in a medium mixing bowl.

In a separate bowl, mix the rice and yogurt.

Season both mixtures with sea salt and freshly ground pepper to taste.

Heat the tortillas in a dry nonstick skillet.

Spread each tortilla with the avocado mixture, and top with the rice, cilantro, and onion, followed by the asparagus.

Fold up both sides of the tortilla, and roll tightly to close. Cut in half diagonally before serving.

Serves 6.

Beef Gyros

Classic Greek gyros are often made from lamb, but these beef gyros are easy and delicious. Using pita bread minimizes the carbohydrates in this sandwich. You could also make this with leftover lean roast beef.

For the tzatziki:
- 2 cups Greek yogurt
- 3 tablespoons lemon juice
- 4 cloves garlic, minced
- 1 medium cucumber, peeled, seeded, and grated
- 1/2 teaspoon cumin
- 4–5 mint leaves, chopped
- Sea salt and freshly ground pepper, to taste

For the marinade:
- 1/2 onion, quartered
- 1/4 cup water
- 3 cloves garlic
- 2 tablespoons sugar
- 1 teaspoon prepared mustard
- 1 teaspoon freshly ground pepper
- 1 tablespoon olive oil
- 1/2 teaspoon ground ginger
- 1/2 teaspoon cayenne pepper

For the filling:
- 1 1/2 pounds sirloin tip roast cut into 1-inch strips
- 1 package pita bread
- 1 head romaine, chopped into ribbons
- 2 tomatoes, chopped
- 1 red onion, thinly sliced

Make the tzatziki:

Stir together the yogurt, lemon juice, garlic, cucumber, cumin, and mint in a small bowl until smooth.

Season with sea salt and freshly ground pepper to taste.

Make the marinade:

Combine all the marinade ingredients in a food processor and process until smooth.

Place the marinade in a plastic bag or shallow dish.

Make the filling:

Place the beef in the marinade and refrigerate for at least 4 hours, or overnight. Drain.

Grill meat in a grill basket over medium-high heat for 6–8 minutes, or until cooked through. Remove from the heat.

Warm pita bread on the grill, or in a toaster oven.

Place some of the cooked meat inside the pita. Top with the lettuce, tomato, red onion, and cucumber sauce.

Serve the gyros with a green salad or roasted potatoes.

Serves 6.

Cucumber Basil Sandwiches

The addition of basil adds antioxidants and flavor to this hummus sandwich. The skin and seeds of the cucumber contain many nutrients, so don't remove them. If you like, make it an open-faced sandwich to further reduce the carbohydrates and calories.

- 4 slices whole-grain bread
- 1/4 cup hummus
- 1 large cucumber, thinly sliced
- 4 whole basil leaves

Spread the hummus on 2 slices of bread, and layer the cucumbers onto it.

Top with the basil leaves and close the sandwiches.

Press down lightly and serve immediately.

Serves 2.

Falafel

Falafel is a traditional Middle Eastern food thought to have originated in Egypt, but it is considered the national dish of Israel. It is made from chickpeas, which are a good source of fiber and protein. Add any vegetables you'd like to the finished sandwich, such as cucumbers or shredded lettuce.

For the tahini sauce:

- 1/2 cup tahini sauce
- 1/4 cup flat-leaf parsley, finely chopped
- 2 tablespoons lemon juice
- 2 cloves garlic, minced
- 1/2 cup cold water, as needed

For the falafel:

- 1 cup dried chickpeas, soaked overnight
- 1 large onion, chopped
- 1/4 cup flat-leaf parsley, chopped
- 1/4 cup cilantro, chopped
- 4 cloves garlic, peeled
- 1 teaspoon sea salt
- 1 teaspoon cumin
- 1/2 teaspoon chili flakes
- 1 1/2 teaspoons baking soda, dissolved in 1 teaspoon water
- 4–6 tablespoons flour
- 2 cups peanut oil
- 1 tomato, chopped
- 1 bell pepper, chopped
- 4 pita rounds

Make the tahini sauce:

Whisk the tahini, parsley, lemon juice, and garlic together until creamy. Add up to 1/2 cup cold water as needed to thin the sauce and make it smooth and creamy.

Cover and refrigerate while you make the falafel.

Make the falafel:

Drain the chickpeas and add them to a large food processor with the onion, parsley, cilantro, garlic, sea salt, cumin, and chili flakes.

Process until well mixed but not pureed, then add the baking soda and flour, and pulse until a rough dough forms. (The dough should hold together and not stick to your hands. Add flour as needed to keep dough from being too tacky.)

Cover dough in a large bowl and refrigerate for several hours.

Form the dough into small balls the size of walnuts.

Heat 3 inches of oil to 375 degrees in a large pot.

Fry one ball and see if it holds together. If the ball falls apart, add more flour to the dough.

Once proper consistency has been achieved, fry the chickpea balls 6 at a time, turning to make sure they are golden brown on all sides, and drain on a paper towel.

Stuff pitas with falafel balls, garnish with tomatoes and bell peppers, and drizzle with tahini sauce.

Serves 4.

Greek Salad Pita

Greek salad is a healthful and satisfying mélange of cheese and vegetables. It becomes even more convenient and filling when served in pita bread. Seek out high-quality, low-fat feta that's not too high in sodium.

- 1 cup chopped romaine lettuce
- 1 tomato, chopped and seeded
- 1/2 cup baby spinach leaves
- 1/2 small red onion, thinly sliced
- 1/2 small cucumber, chopped and seeded
- 2 tablespoons olive oil
- 1 tablespoon crumbled feta cheese
- 1/2 tablespoon red wine vinegar
- 1 teaspoon Dijon mustard
- Sea salt and freshly ground pepper, to taste
- 1 whole-wheat pita

Combine everything except the sea salt, freshly ground pepper, and pita bread in a medium bowl.

Toss until the salad is well combined.

Season with sea salt and freshly ground pepper to taste.

Fill the pita with the salad mixture, serve, and enjoy!

Serves 4.

Grilled Chicken Salad Pita

Tender and juicy grilled chicken topped with fresh vegetables in a pita pocket makes a filling and hearty meal. Serve this with celery and carrot sticks on the side for crunch instead of salty chips.

- 1 boneless, skinless chicken breast
- Sea salt and freshly ground pepper, to taste
- 1 cup baby spinach
- 1 roasted red pepper, sliced
- 1 tomato, chopped
- 1/2 small red onion, thinly sliced
- 1/2 small cucumber, chopped
- 4 tablespoons olive oil
- Juice of 1 lemon
- 1 whole-wheat pita pocket
- 2 tablespoons crumbled feta cheese

Preheat a gas or charcoal grill to medium-high heat.

Season the chicken breast with sea salt and freshly ground pepper, and grill until cooked through, about 7–8 minutes per side.

Allow chicken to rest for 5 minutes before slicing into strips.

While the chicken is cooking, put all the chopped vegetables into a medium-mixing bowl and season with sea salt and freshly ground pepper.

Chop the chicken into cubes and add to salad.

Add the olive oil and lemon juice and toss well.

Stuff the mixture onto a pita pocket and top with the feta cheese. Serve immediately.

Serves 1.

Grilled Eggplant and Feta Sandwiches

The classic combination of eggplant and feta is popular in many Greek dishes. Grilled slices of eggplant replace deli meats, and hummus adds protein and fiber while taking the place of mayonnaise.

- 1 medium eggplant, sliced into 1/2-inch-thick slices
- 2 tablespoons olive oil
- Sea salt and freshly ground pepper, to taste
- 5–6 tablespoons hummus
- 4 slices whole-wheat bread, toasted
- 1 cup baby spinach leaves
- 2 ounces feta cheese, softened

Preheat a gas or charcoal grill to medium-high heat.

Salt both sides of the sliced eggplant, and let sit for 20 minutes to draw out the bitter juices.

Rinse the eggplant and pat dry with a paper towel.

Brush the eggplant slices with olive oil and season with sea salt and freshly ground pepper.

Grill the eggplant until lightly charred on both sides but still slightly firm in the middle, about 3–4 minutes a side.

Spread the hummus on the bread and top with the spinach leaves, feta, and eggplant. Top with the other slice of bread and serve warm.

Serves 2.

Mediterranean Tuna Salad Sandwiches

Usually loaded with high-fat mayonnaise, tuna salad does not often come to mind as a healthful staple. This version is made with Greek yogurt and flavorful roasted peppers, adding taste and moisture without a lot of fat. You can also enjoy the tuna salad without the bread, if you prefer.

- 1 can white tuna, packed in water or olive oil, drained
- 1 roasted red pepper, diced
- 1/2 small red onion, diced
- 10 low-salt olives, pitted and finely chopped
- 1/4 cup plain Greek yogurt
- 1 tablespoon flat-leaf parsley, chopped
- Juice of 1 lemon
- Sea salt and freshly ground pepper, to taste
- 4 whole-grain pieces of bread

In a small bowl, combine all of the ingredients except the bread, and mix well.

Season with sea salt and freshly ground pepper to taste.

Toast the bread or warm in a pan.

Make the sandwich and serve immediately.

Serves 2.

Open-Faced Eggplant Parmesan Sandwich

Eggplant Parmesan is often deep fried, laden with high-fat cheese, and served with mounds of pasta. In this version, the eggplant is broiled before being topped with marinara and low-fat Parmesan cheese, and served on a slice of toasted whole-grain bread. Eat with a knife and fork!

- 1 small eggplant, sliced into 1/4-inch rounds
- Pinch sea salt
- 2 tablespoons olive oil
- Sea salt and freshly ground pepper, to taste
- 2 slices whole-grain bread, thickly cut and toasted
- 1 cup marinara sauce (no added sugar)
- 1/4 cup freshly grated, low-fat Parmesan cheese

Preheat broiler to high heat.

Salt both sides of the sliced eggplant, and let sit for 20 minutes to draw out the bitter juices.

Rinse the eggplant and pat dry with a paper towel.

Brush the eggplant with the olive oil, and season with sea salt and freshly ground pepper.

Lay the eggplant on a sheet pan, and broil until crisp, about 4 minutes. Flip over and crisp the other side.

Lay the toasted bread on a sheet pan. Spoon some marinara sauce on each slice of bread, and layer the eggplant on top.

Sprinkle half of the cheese on top of the eggplant and top with more marinara sauce.

Sprinkle with remaining cheese.

Put the sandwiches under the broiler until the cheese has melted, about 2 minutes.

Using a spatula, transfer the sandwiches to plates and serve.

Serves 2.

Open-Faced Grilled Caesar Salad Sandwiches

Caesar salad may be a West Coast invention, but it includes many classic ingredients of the Mediterranean. Here the classic salad is grilled, then made into a sandwich. Enjoy it with fresh fruit on the side.

- 3/4 cup olive oil, divided
- 2 romaine hearts, left intact
- 3–4 anchovy filets
- Juice of 1 lemon
- 2–3 cloves garlic, peeled
- 1 teaspoon Dijon mustard
- 1/4 teaspoon Worcestershire sauce
- Sea salt and freshly ground pepper, to taste
- 2 slices whole-wheat bread, toasted
- Freshly grated, low-fat Parmesan cheese

Heat a grill over medium-high heat. Oil the grates.

On a cutting board, drizzle the lettuce with 1–2 tablespoons of olive oil and place on the grates.

Grill for 5 minutes, turning until lettuce is slightly charred on all sides.

Let lettuce cool enough to handle.

In a food processor, combine the rest of the olive oil with the anchovies, lemon juice, garlic, mustard, and Worcestershire sauce.

Pulse all ingredients until you have a smooth emulsion.

Season with sea salt and freshly ground pepper to taste.

Chop the lettuce in half and place on the bread.

Drizzle with the dressing and top with the Parmesan cheese.

Serve and enjoy!

Serves 2.

Slow-Roasted Tomato and Basil Panini

Slow roasting tomatoes brings out their flavor, and cooking them actually increases their lycopene. Here the flavors of an Italian Caprese salad are transformed into a sandwich. If you don't have a panini maker or grill pan, you can easily toast the sandwich in a nonstick skillet.

- 4 Roma tomatoes, halved
- 4 cloves garlic
- 2 tablespoons olive oil
- 1 tablespoon Italian seasoning
- Sea salt and freshly ground pepper, to taste
- 4 basil leaves
- 2 slices fresh mozzarella
- 4 slices whole-grain bread

Preheat oven to 250 degrees.

Lay the tomatoes and garlic cloves on a sheet pan, and drizzle with the olive oil.

Sprinkle with Italian seasoning, and season with the sea salt and freshly ground pepper.

Roast for about 2 1/2–3 hours, until tomatoes are extremely fragrant and slightly wilted.

To make the panini, layer the tomatoes with the basil and cheese on the bread.

Preheat a panini maker, and cook the sandwiches until the bread is browned and the cheese is melted.

If you don't have a panini maker, just heat a grill pan on medium-high heat, and place the sandwich directly on the grill pan. Place another pan on top to press the sandwich.

Flip the panini after 3–4 minutes when the bread has nice grill marks, and cook the other side.

Serve warm.

Serves 2.

Spinach and Mushroom Pita

This easy-to-put-together pita pocket makes a light and healthful lunch option. Lemon is a key ingredient in the south of France, as well as in Italy, Spain, and Greece; use it to add flavor and freshness to salads and sandwiches. All of the ingredients in the sandwich can also be used in salads, so stock up your refrigerator produce drawer!

- 2 cups baby spinach leaves
- 1 small red onion, thinly sliced
- 1/2 cup button mushrooms, sliced
- 1/2 cup alfalfa sprouts
- 1 tomato, chopped
- 1/2 small cucumber
- 2 tablespoons olive oil
- Juice of 1 lemon
- Sea salt and freshly ground pepper, to taste
- 2 whole-grain pita pockets

Combine all the vegetables, olive oil, and lemon juice in a bowl, and season with sea salt and freshly ground pepper to taste.

Toss the salad until well mixed.

Stuff the vegetable mixture into the pita pockets and serve immediately.

Serves 2.

7

GRAINS AND PASTAS

- Apple Couscous with Curry
- Baked Ziti
- Brown Rice with Apricots, Cherries, and Toasted Pecans
- Couscous with Apricots
- Crunchy Pea and Barley Salad
- Cumin-Scented Lentils with Rice
- Herbed Barley
- Penne with Broccoli and Anchovies
- Quinoa, Broccoli, and Baby Potatoes
- Rice and Lentils
- Rice Pilaf
- Skillet Bulgur with Kale and Tomatoes
- Spicy Broccoli Pasta Salad
- Walnut Spaghetti
- Wild Mushroom Risotto

Apple Couscous with Curry

Couscous is originally a North African Berber dish, but now is common in Libya, Morocco, Tunisia, Algeria, and France. This dish has a complex variety of sweet and savory flavors. The light and fluffy couscous is stuffed with crunchy chopped nuts, but feel free to substitute walnuts or pistachios for the pecans.

- 2 teaspoons olive oil
- 2 leeks, white parts only, sliced
- 1 Granny Smith apple, diced
- 2 cups cooked whole-wheat couscous
- 2 tablespoons curry powder
- 1/2 cup chopped pecans

Heat the olive oil in a large skillet on medium heat and add leeks. Cook until soft and tender, about 5 minutes.

Add diced apple and cook until soft.

Add couscous and curry powder, then stir to combine.

Remove from heat, mix in nuts, and serve.

Serves 4.

Baked Ziti

Baked ziti is an American classic and the perfect dish for potlucks. Using whole-wheat pasta, low-fat cheeses, and homemade marinara sauce makes it healthier and lighter. It can also be assembled ahead of time and baked at the last minute, and it's easy to double or even triple the recipe for large groups.

For the marinara sauce:
- 2 tablespoons olive oil
- 1/4 medium onion, diced (about 3 tablespoons)
- 3 cloves garlic, chopped
- 1 (28-ounce) can whole, peeled tomatoes, roughly chopped
- Sprig of fresh thyme
- 1/2 bunch fresh basil
- Sea salt and freshly ground pepper, to taste

For the ziti:
- 1 pound whole-wheat ziti
- 3 1/2 cups marinara sauce
- 1 cup low-fat cottage cheese
- 1 cup grated, low-fat mozzarella cheese, divided
- 3/4 cup freshly grated, low-fat Parmesan cheese, divided

Make the marinara sauce:

Heat the olive oil in a medium saucepan over medium-high heat.

Sauté the onion and garlic, stirring until lightly browned, about 3 minutes.

Add the tomatoes and the herb sprigs, and bring to a boil.

Lower the heat and simmer, covered, for 10 minutes.

Remove and discard the herb sprigs.

Stir in sea salt and season with freshly ground pepper to taste.

Make the ziti:

Preheat the oven to 375 degrees.

Prepare the pasta according to package directions. Drain pasta.

Combine the pasta in a bowl with 2 cups marinara sauce, the cottage cheese, and half the mozzarella and Parmesan cheeses.

Spread the mixture in a baking dish, and top with the remaining marinara sauce and cheese.

Bake for 30–40 minutes, or until bubbly and golden brown.

Serves 8.

Brown Rice with Apricots, Cherries, and Toasted Pecans

While not a traditional Mediterranean ingredient, brown rice is a great source of fiber and combines easily with lots of other healthful additions. The dried apricots and cherries add tartness to this dish, while the pecans add crunch and extra flavor. If you prefer, use pistachios, walnuts, or almonds in place of the pecans.

- 2 tablespoons olive oil
- 2 green onions, sliced
- 1/2 cup brown rice
- 1 cup chicken stock
- 4–5 dried apricots, chopped
- 2 tablespoons dried cherries
- 2 tablespoons pecans, toasted and chopped
- Sea salt and freshly ground pepper, to taste

Heat the olive oil in a medium saucepan, and add the green onions.

Sauté for 1–2 minutes, and add the rice. Stir to coat in oil, then add the stock.

Bring to a boil, reduce heat, and cover.

Simmer for 50 minutes.

Remove the lid, add the apricots, cherries, and pecans, and cover for 10 more minutes.

Fluff with a fork to mix the fruit into the rice, season with sea salt and freshly ground pepper, and serve.

Serves 2.

Couscous with Apricots

This vegetarian dish is as pretty as it is delicious. Including dried fruits and nuts adds a nutritious boost. Serve with roasted pork loin or chicken, or eat it by itself.

- 2 tablespoons olive oil
- 1 small onion, diced
- 1 cup whole-wheat couscous
- 2 cups water or broth
- 1/2 cup dried apricots, soaked in water overnight
- 1/2 cup slivered almonds or pistachios
- 1/2 teaspoon dried mint
- 1/2 teaspoon dried thyme

Heat the olive oil in a large skillet over medium-high heat. Add the onion and cook until translucent and soft.

Stir in the couscous and cook for 2–3 minutes.

Add the water or broth, cover, and cook for 8–10 minutes until the water is mostly absorbed.

Remove from the heat and let stand for a few minutes.

Fluff with a fork and fold in the apricots, nuts, mint, and thyme.

Serves 4.

Crunchy Pea and Barley Salad

Whole grains are an important part of the Mediterranean diet. Quick-cooking barley doesn't take long to prepare and is loaded with fiber and antioxidants. Served on its own, this salad makes a filling vegetarian meal, but it also works as a side dish.

- 2 cups water
- 1 cup quick-cooking barley
- 2 cups sugar snap pea pods
- Small bunch flat-leaf parsley, chopped
- 1/2 small red onion, diced
- 2 tablespoons olive oil
- Juice of 1 lemon
- Sea salt and freshly ground pepper, to taste

Bring water to boil in a saucepan. Stir in the barley and cover.

Simmer for 10 minutes until all water is absorbed, and then let stand about 5 minutes covered.

Rinse the barley under cold water and combine it with the peas, parsley, onion, olive oil, and lemon juice.

Season with sea salt and freshly ground pepper to taste.

Serves 4.

Cumin-Scented Lentils with Rice

This classic Lebanese dish, called megadarra, pairs well with chicken, lamb, or fish.

- 1/4 cup olive oil
- 1 medium onion, thinly sliced
- 1 tablespoon ground cumin
- 1 cup green lentils
- 2 cups water, divided
- 3/4 cup long-grain rice, rinsed
- 2 bay leaves
- Sea salt and freshly ground pepper, to taste

Heat a large saucepan over medium heat.

Add the olive oil and onion, and sauté for 10 minutes until soft and translucent.

Add the cumin and stir to incorporate.

Add the lentils and stir to coat in the oil.

Add 1 cup water, bring to a boil, and reduce to a simmer.

Simmer for 15 minutes, until most of the water has been absorbed.

Add the rice to the pot, along with remaining 1 cup water and the bay leaves, and bring to a boil.

Reduce heat, cover and simmer for 15–20 more minutes, checking periodically and adding water to prevent rice or lentils from becoming scorched.

When both the rice and lentils are tender and cooked through, stir and season with sea salt and freshly ground pepper.

Remove the bay leaves and serve immediately.

Serves 2.

Herbed Barley

Barley was one of the first cultivated grains from the Fertile Crescent, a region that encompasses modern Israel, Iraq, Syria, Lebanon, and Palestine. It's a good source of dietary fiber. Serve this dish with roasted chicken instead of rice.

- 2 tablespoons olive oil
- 1/2 cup diced onion
- 1/2 cup diced celery
- 1 carrot, peeled and diced
- 3 cups water or chicken broth
- 1 cup barley
- 1 bay leaf
- 1/2 teaspoon thyme
- 1/2 teaspoon rosemary
- 1/4 cup walnuts or pine nuts
- Sea salt and freshly ground pepper, to taste

Heat the olive oil in a medium saucepan over medium-high heat. Sauté the onion, celery, and carrot over medium heat until they are tender.

Add the water or chicken broth, barley, and seasonings, and bring to a boil. Reduce the heat and simmer for 25 minutes, or until tender.

Stir in the nuts and season to taste.

Serves 4.

Penne with Broccoli and Anchovies

In Italy, broccoli rabe is used in this dish, but regular broccoli works just as well. The combination of broccoli, roasted garlic, and anchovies gives this dish a rich, savory flavor and plenty of antioxidants. Skip the Parmesan cheese if you want to reduce calories.

- 1/4 cup olive oil
- 1 pound whole-wheat pasta
- 1/2 pound broccoli or broccoli rabe cut into 1-inch florets
- 3–4 anchovy filets, packed in olive oil
- 2 cloves garlic, sliced
- Pinch red pepper flakes
- 1/4 cup freshly grated, low-fat Parmesan
- Sea salt and freshly ground pepper, to taste

Heat the olive oil in a deep skillet on medium heat.

In the meantime, prepare the pasta al dente, according to the package directions.

Fry the broccoli, anchovies, and garlic in the oil until the broccoli is almost tender and the garlic is slightly browned, about 5 minutes or so.

Rinse and drain the pasta, and add it to the broccoli mixture.

Stir to coat the pasta with the garlic oil.

Transfer to a serving dish, toss with red pepper flakes and Parmesan, and season.

Serves 4.

Quinoa, Broccoli, and Baby Potatoes

Originally from the Andes, quinoa is a starch that's quick and easy to cook as well as extremely healthful: it's high in manganese, magnesium, protein, and more. Before cooking quinoa be sure to rinse it; otherwise, it may have a bitter flavor.

- 2 tablespoons olive oil
- 1 cup baby potatoes, cut in half
- 1 cup broccoli florets
- 2 cups cooked quinoa
- Zest of 1 lemon
- Sea salt and freshly ground pepper, to taste

Heat the olive oil in a large skillet.

Add the potatoes and cook until tender and golden brown.

Add the broccoli and cook until soft, about 3 minutes.

Remove from heat and add the quinoa and lemon zest. Season and serve.

Serves 4.

Rice and Lentils

Rice and lentils are traditionally paired in many Mediterranean cuisines. Here, brown rice is used instead of the classic white rice. This version has a touch of sweetness from the caramelized onions. Cook the onions very slowly, stirring frequently so they caramelize and don't burn.

- 2 cups green or brown lentils
- 1 cup brown rice
- 5 cups water or chicken stock
- 1/2 teaspoon sea salt
- 1/2 teaspoon freshly ground pepper
- 1/2 teaspoon dried thyme
- 1/4 cup olive oil
- 3 onions, peeled and sliced

Place the lentils and rice in a large saucepan with water or chicken stock. Bring to a boil, cover, and simmer for 20–25 minutes, or until almost tender.

Add the seasonings and cook an additional 20–30 minutes, or until the rice is tender and the water is absorbed.

In another saucepan, heat the olive oil over medium heat. Add the onions and cook very slowly, stirring frequently, until the onions become browned and caramelized, about 20 minutes.

To serve, ladle the lentils and rice into bowls and top with the caramelized onions.

Serves 4.

Rice Pilaf

Pilaf is a type of rice dish that pairs well with meats, fish, and poultry. This dish is seasoned traditionally with cinnamon and raisins, but you can omit these, if you prefer.

- 2 tablespoons olive oil
- 1 medium onion, diced
- 1/4 cup pine nuts
- 1 1/2 cups long-grain brown rice
- 2 1/2 cups hot chicken stock
- 1 cinnamon stick
- 1/4 cup raisins
- Sea salt and freshly ground pepper, to taste

Heat the olive oil in a large saucepan over medium heat.

Sauté the onions and pine nuts for 6–8 minutes, or until the pine nuts are golden and the onion is translucent.

Add the rice and sauté for 2 minutes until lightly browned.

Pour the chicken stock into the pan and bring to a boil.

Add the cinnamon and raisins.

Lower the heat, cover the pan, and simmer for 15–20 minutes, or until the rice is tender and the liquid is absorbed.

Remove from the heat and fluff with a fork. Season and serve.

Serves 6.

Skillet Bulgur with Kale and Tomatoes

Originally from the Middle East, bulgur is high in protein and fiber. A great side dish, it can be served with roast chicken or fish.

- 2 tablespoons olive oil
- 2 cloves garlic, minced
- 1 bunch kale, trimmed and cut into bite-sized pieces
- Juice of 1 lemon
- 2 cups cooked bulgur wheat
- 1 pint cherry tomatoes, halved
- Sea salt and freshly ground pepper, to taste

Heat the olive oil in a large skillet over medium heat. Add the garlic and sauté for 1 minute.

Add the kale leaves and stir to coat. Cook for 5 minutes until leaves are cooked through and thoroughly wilted.

Add the lemon juice, then the bulgur and tomatoes.

Season with sea salt and freshly ground pepper.

Serves 2.

Spicy Broccoli Pasta Salad

Broccoli can help lower cholesterol, and it's high in vitamins C and K, as well as folate. This salad is perfect for picnics or potlucks.

- 8 ounces whole-wheat pasta
- 2 cups broccoli florets
- 1 cup carrots, peeled and shredded
- 1/4 cup plain Greek yogurt
- Juice of 1 lemon
- 1 teaspoon red pepper flakes
- Sea salt and freshly ground pepper, to taste

Cook the pasta according to the package directions for al dente and drain well.

When the pasta is cool, combine it with the veggies, yogurt, lemon juice, and red pepper flakes in a large bowl, and stir thoroughly to combine.

Taste for seasoning, and add sea salt and freshly ground pepper as needed.

This dish can be served at room temperature or chilled.

Serves 2.

Walnut Spaghetti

This delicious, simple dish is traditionally served around Christmastime in Naples, Italy, but it's so easy you'll want to make it all year round! In addition to being tasty, walnuts are high in antioxidants and healthful fats. Toast the walnuts until lightly brown, but don't burn them.

- 1 pound whole-wheat spaghetti
- 1/2 cup olive oil
- 4 cloves garlic, minced
- 3/4 cup walnuts, toasted and finely chopped
- 2 tablespoons low-fat ricotta cheese
- 1/2 cup freshly grated, low-fat Parmesan cheese
- 1/4 cup flat-leaf parsley, chopped
- Sea salt and freshly ground pepper, to taste

Prepare the spaghetti in boiling water according to package directions for al dente, reserving 1 cup of the pasta water.

Heat the olive oil in a large skillet on medium-low heat.

Add the garlic and sauté for 1–2 minutes.

Ladle 1/2 cup of the pasta water into the skillet, and continue to simmer for 5–10 minutes.

Add the chopped walnuts and ricotta cheese.

Toss the walnut sauce with the spaghetti in a large serving bowl.

Top with the Parmesan cheese and parsley. Season and serve.

Serves 6.

Wild Mushroom Risotto

Risotto is a type of Italian starchy rice dish that cooks into a creamy consistency. It is classically paired with earthy wild mushrooms and Parmesan cheese. Serve it as a first course, or as a side dish with chicken or pork.

- 2 ounces dried porcini mushrooms
- 5 cups chicken stock
- 2 tablespoons olive oil
- 1 small onion, minced
- 2 cups brown rice
- 1/2 cup freshly grated, low-fat Parmesan cheese
- Sea salt and freshly ground pepper, to taste

Place the mushrooms in a bowl and cover them with hot water. Set them aside for 30 minutes. Drain them, reserving the liquid, and wash them.

Strain the liquid through a sieve lined with cheesecloth.

Add the liquid to the chicken stock.

Heat the chicken stock and mushroom liquid in a small saucepan. When simmering, turn heat to lowest setting.

Heat the olive oil in a large saucepan over medium heat.

Add the onion and sauté for 3–5 minutes, or until tender.

Stir in the rice and mushrooms and 3/4 cup of the stock.

Continue cooking the rice, stirring almost constantly, and adding more liquid, a ladleful at a time, as soon as the rice absorbs the liquid. There should always be some liquid visible in the pan.

Cook, adding liquid every few minutes, until the rice is tender, with a slightly firm center, 20–30 minutes.

Remove from the heat, and stir in the Parmesan cheese, a spoonful at a time.

Season to taste and serve.

Serves 6.

8

POULTRY DISHES

- Arroz con Pollo
- Braised Chicken with Wild Mushrooms
- Braised Duck with Fennel Root
- Chicken and Potato Tagine
- Chicken Marsala
- Chicken Tagine with Olives
- Citrus Chicken with Pecan Wild Rice
- Grilled Chicken and Vegetables with Lemon-Walnut Sauce
- Lebanese Grilled Chicken
- Marinated Chicken
- Niçoise Chicken
- Pomegranate-Glazed Chicken
- Roast Chicken
- Roasted Cornish Hen with Figs

Arroz con Pollo

Although this rice is generally thought of as a Latin American dish, you'll find it in Spain as well. This dish is easy to prepare and can be adapted to your taste. Add more vegetables, such as artichokes or peas, to boost fiber and decrease calories.

- 4 tablespoons olive oil
- 1 chicken, cut into pieces
- Sea salt and freshly ground pepper, to taste
- 3 sweet red peppers, coarsely chopped
- 1 onion, chopped
- 2 garlic cloves, minced
- 2 1/2 cups chicken stock
- 1 (14-ounce) can diced tomatoes, drained
- 1 tablespoon paprika
- 1 cup brown rice
- 1/4 cup flat-leaf parsley, chopped

Heat the olive oil in a large skillet on medium-high heat.

Place the chicken in the pan, and cook it 8–10 minutes, or until lightly browned on both sides.

Transfer the chicken to an oven-safe dish, and keep warm in the oven on the lowest setting.

Add sea salt and freshly ground pepper to taste.

Add the sweet peppers, onion, and garlic to the pan, and cook, stirring frequently, until tender.

Heat the chicken stock in the microwave or a saucepan until simmering.

Add the chicken stock, tomatoes, and paprika to the pan.

Stir in the rice, and place the chicken pieces on top.

Simmer with the lid on for 20–30 minutes, or until the liquid is absorbed and the rice is tender.

Garnish with parsley.

Serve with a green salad or tomato and red onion salad.

Serves 6.

Braised Chicken with Wild Mushrooms

This Italian stew is hearty and satisfying, and can be served with a variety of vegetables or salads. Stews improve with time, so make this the night before you want to serve it.

- 1/4 cup dried porcini or morel mushrooms
- 1/4 cup olive oil
- 2–3 slices low-salt turkey bacon, chopped
- 1 chicken, cut into pieces
- Sea salt and freshly ground pepper, to taste
- 1 small celery stalk, diced
- 1 small dried red chili, chopped
- 1/4 cup vermouth or white wine
- 1/4 cup tomato puree
- 1/4 cup low-salt chicken stock
- 1/2 teaspoon arrowroot
- 1/4 cup flat-leaf parsley, chopped
- 4 teaspoons fresh thyme, chopped
- 3 teaspoons fresh tarragon

Place the mushrooms in a small bowl and pour boiling water over them. Allow them to stand for 20 minutes to soften.

Drain and chop, reserving the liquid.

Heat the olive oil in a heavy stew pot on medium heat.

Add the bacon and cook until browned and slightly crisp.

Drain the bacon on a paper towel.

Season the chicken with sea salt and freshly ground pepper, and add to the oil and bacon drippings.

Cook for 10–15 minutes, turning halfway through the cooking time so that both sides of the chicken are golden brown.

Add the celery and the chopped chili, and cook for 3–5 minutes or until soft.

Deglaze the pan with the wine, using a wooden spoon to scrape up the brown bits stuck to the bottom.

Add the tomato puree, chicken stock, arrowroot, and mushroom liquid.

Cover and simmer on low for 45 minutes.

Add the fresh chopped herbs and cook an additional 10 minutes, until the sauce thickens.

Season with sea salt and freshly ground pepper to taste.

Serve with wilted greens or crunchy green beans.

Serves 4.

Braised Duck with Fennel Root

Roasted or braised fennel is sweet and mild, and fennel provides a great source of vitamin C, fiber, and potassium. It pairs perfectly with the rich taste of duck, but you can also use chicken, which is leaner and lower in calories.

- 1/4 cup olive oil
- 1 whole duck, cleaned
- 3 teaspoon fresh rosemary
- 2 garlic cloves, minced
- Sea salt and freshly ground pepper, to taste
- 3 fennel bulbs, cut into chunks
- 1/2 cup sherry

Preheat the oven to 375 degrees.

Heat the olive oil in a large stew pot or Dutch oven.

Season the duck, including the cavity, with the rosemary, garlic, sea salt, and freshly ground pepper.

Place the duck in the oil, and cook it for 10–15 minutes, turning as necessary to brown all sides.

Add the fennel bulbs and cook an additional 5 minutes.

Pour the sherry over the duck and fennel, cover the pot, and cook in the oven for 30–45 minutes, or until internal temperature of the duck is 140–150 degrees at its thickest part.

Allow duck to sit for 15 minutes before serving.

Serves 6.

Chicken and Potato Tagine

The term "tagine" refers to both the cooking vessel and the finished dish. Use a Dutch oven or casserole dish if you don't have a tagine. Small amounts of meat and poultry are balanced with large servings of vegetables on this diet.

- 1 chicken, cut up into 8 pieces
- 1 medium onion, thinly sliced
- 3 cloves garlic, minced
- 1/4 cup olive oil
- 1/2 teaspoon ground cumin
- 1/2 teaspoon freshly ground pepper
- 1/4 teaspoon ginger
- Pinch saffron threads
- 1 teaspoon paprika
- Sea salt, to taste
- 2 cups water
- 3 cups potatoes, peeled and diced
- 1/2 cup flat-leaf parsley, chopped
- 1/2 cup fresh cilantro, chopped
- 1 cup fresh or frozen green peas

Place the chicken, onion, garlic, olive oil, and seasonings into a Dutch oven.

Add about 2 cups water and bring to a boil over medium-high heat.

Reduce heat and cover. Simmer for 30 minutes.

Add the potatoes, parsley, and cilantro, and simmer an additional 20 minutes, or until the potatoes are almost tender.

Add the peas at the last moment, simmering for an additional 5 minutes.

Serve hot.

Serves 6.

Chicken Marsala

The secret to this Italian classic is to pound the chicken breasts thin between two pieces of wax paper, so they cook quickly and evenly. Small servings of meat and large portions of vegetables are easy to achieve with this entrée.

- 1/4 cup olive oil
- 4 boneless, skinless chicken breasts, pounded thin
- Sea salt and freshly ground pepper, to taste
- 1/4 cup whole-wheat flour
- 1/2 pound mushrooms, sliced
- 1 cup Marsala wine
- 1 cup chicken broth
- 1/4 cup flat-leaf parsley, chopped

Heat the olive oil in a large skillet on medium-high heat.

Season the chicken breasts with sea salt and freshly ground pepper, then dredge them in flour.

Sauté them in the olive oil until golden brown.

Transfer to an oven-safe plate, and keep warm in the oven on low.

Sauté the mushrooms in the same pan. Add the wine and chicken broth and bring to a simmer.

Simmer for 10 minutes, or until the sauce is reduced and thickened slightly.

Return the chicken to the pan, and cook it in the sauce for 10 minutes.

Transfer to a serving dish and sprinkle with the parsley.

Serves 4.

Chicken Tagine with Olives

Tagine is a traditional Moroccan stew. This version gets its bright color from saffron and turmeric. Use a combination of purple and green pitted olives if you can find them. Olives are a key component of the Mediterranean diet, and are a good source of vitamin E.

- 1 teaspoon ground ginger
- 1/2 teaspoon ground cumin
- 1/2 teaspoon paprika
- 1/2 teaspoon turmeric
- Pinch saffron threads
- 1 clove garlic, minced
- 1 whole chicken
- 2 medium onions, thinly sliced
- 1/2 cup finely chopped flat-leaf parsley
- 1/2 cup finely chopped cilantro
- 1 cinnamon stick
- 3 cups water
- 2 tablespoons olive oil
- 1 tablespoon butter
- Juice and zest of 1 lemon
- 1 cup green or purple olives (or a combination of both), pitted
- Sea salt and freshly ground pepper, to taste

Combine the spices and garlic in a small bowl.

Pat the chicken dry, brush the spices over the chicken, and massage them in with your fingers, including in the cavity.

Place the chicken in a large stew pot or Dutch oven.

Add the onions, parsley, cilantro, and cinnamon stick to the pot along with the water.

Bring the water to a boil and add the olive oil, butter, and lemon zest and juice.

Cover and simmer for 1–2 hours, or until the chicken is tender and the sauce has reduced and thickened slightly.

Remove the lid and simmer an additional 15 minutes. Season with sea salt and freshly ground pepper to taste.

Add the olives immediately before serving.

Serves 6.

Citrus Chicken with Pecan Wild Rice

While not traditionally from the region, this combination of orange, healthful nuts, and wild rice fits well with the Mediterranean diet. Wild rice is a good source of fiber, zinc, iron, and vitamins B1, B2, B3, and B9.

- 4 boneless, skinless chicken breasts
- Sea salt and freshly ground pepper, to taste
- 2 tablespoons olive oil
- Juice and zest of 1 orange
- 2 cups wild rice, cooked
- 2 green onions, sliced
- 1 cup pecans, toasted and chopped

Season chicken breasts with sea salt and freshly ground pepper.

Heat a large skillet over medium heat. Add the oil and sear the chicken until browned on 1 side.

Flip the chicken and brown other side.

Add the orange juice to the skillet and let cook down.

In a large bowl, combine the rice, onions, pecans, and orange zest.

Season with sea salt and freshly ground pepper to taste.

Serve the chicken alongside the rice and a green salad for a complete meal.

Serves 4.

Grilled Chicken and Vegetables with Lemon-Walnut Sauce

This grilled chicken and vegetable dish gets a boost from a rich, pureed walnut sauce. While nuts have plenty of omega-3 fatty acids, they are also high in fat, so watch how much sauce you use on each portion. Other vegetables, such as artichokes, carrots, eggplant, or endive, can be used in place of or in addition to the zucchini and asparagus.

- 1 cup chopped walnuts, toasted
- 1 small shallot, very finely chopped
- 1/2 cup olive oil, plus more for brushing
- Juice and zest of 1 lemon
- 4 boneless, skinless chicken breasts
- Sea salt and freshly ground pepper, to taste
- 2 zucchini, sliced diagonally 1/4-inch thick
- 1/2 pound asparagus
- 1 red onion, sliced 1/3-inch thick
- 1 teaspoon Italian seasoning

Preheat a grill to medium-high.

Put the walnuts, shallots, olive oil, lemon juice, and zest in a food processor and process until smooth and creamy.

Season the chicken with sea salt and freshly ground pepper, and grill on an oiled grate until cooked through, about 7–8 minutes a side or until an instant-read thermometer reaches 180 degrees in the thickest part.

When the chicken is halfway done, put the vegetables on the grill.

Sprinkle Italian seasoning over the chicken and vegetables to taste.

To serve, lay the grilled veggies on a plate, place the chicken breast on the grilled vegetables, and spoon the lemon-walnut sauce over the chicken and vegetables.

Serves 4.

Lebanese Grilled Chicken

This grilled chicken is flavored with baharaat, an Arabic spice mix that includes cumin, paprika, coriander, nutmeg, cloves, cinnamon, and black pepper. The chicken must be marinated in these spices for several hours, or overnight. If you are looking to cut calories, use chicken breasts instead of a whole chicken.

- 1/2 cup olive oil
- 1/4 cup apple cider vinegar
- Zest and juice of 1 lemon
- 4 cloves garlic, minced
- 2 teaspoons sea salt
- 1 teaspoon Arabic 7 spices (baharaat)
- 1/2 teaspoon cinnamon
- 1 chicken, cut into 8 pieces

Combine all the ingredients except the chicken in a shallow dish or plastic bag.

Place the chicken in the bag or dish and marinate overnight, or at least for several hours.

Drain, reserving the marinade.

Heat the grill to medium-high.

Cook the chicken pieces for 10–14 minutes, brushing them with the marinade every 5 minutes or so.

The chicken is done when the crust is golden brown and an instant-read thermometer reads 180 degrees in the thickest parts. Remove skin before eating.

Serves 4.

Marinated Chicken

This Italian inspired chicken has a bright, fresh taste from the combination of lemon and rosemary. Lean chicken breasts are a good choice for cutting calories. Make extra to use in salads and sandwiches.

- 1/2 cup olive oil
- 2 tablespoon fresh rosemary
- 1 teaspoon minced garlic
- Juice and zest of 1 lemon
- 1/4 cup chopped flat-leaf parsley
- Sea salt and freshly ground pepper, to taste
- 4 boneless, skinless chicken breasts

Mix all ingredients except the chicken together in a plastic bag or bowl.

Place the chicken in the container and shake/stir so the marinade thoroughly coats the chicken.

Refrigerate up to 24 hours.

Heat a grill to medium heat and cook the chicken for 6–8 minutes a side. Turn only once during the cooking process.

Serve with a Greek salad and brown rice.

Serves 4.

Niçoise Chicken

This dish, inspired by Nice on the French Riviera, makes an easy and elegant meal—simple enough for every day, yet special enough for company. Don't skip the fresh tarragon, which really gives this dish some flair.

- 1/4 cup olive oil
- 3 medium onions, coarsely chopped
- 3 cloves garlic, minced
- 4 pounds chicken breast from 1 cut-up chicken
- 5 Roma tomatoes, peeled and chopped
- 1/2 cup white wine
- 1 (14-1/2 ounce) can chicken broth
- 1/2 cup black Niçoise olives, pitted
- Juice of 1 lemon
- 1/4 cup flat-leaf parsley, chopped
- 1 tablespoon fresh tarragon leaves, chopped
- Sea salt and freshly ground pepper, to taste

Heat the olive oil in a deep saucepan or stew pot over medium heat. Cook the onions and garlic 5 minutes, or until tender and translucent.

Add the chicken and cook an additional 5 minutes to brown slightly.

Add the tomatoes, white wine, and chicken broth, cover, and simmer 30–45 minutes on medium-low heat, or until the chicken is tender and the sauce is thickened slightly.

Remove the lid and add the olives and lemon juice.

Cook an additional 10–15 minutes to thicken the sauce further.

Stir in the parsley and tarragon, and season to taste. Serve immediately with noodles or potatoes and a dark leafy salad.

Serves 6.

Pomegranate-Glazed Chicken

Pomegranates have been grown in the Mediterranean region for a long time and are prominent in many Middle Eastern dishes. In this recipe, the pomegranate juice makes a sweet, fruity glaze for boneless, skinless chicken breasts. From start to finish, this dish takes less than thirty minutes to prepare.

- 1 teaspoon cumin
- 1 clove garlic, minced
- Sea salt and freshly ground pepper, to taste
- 6 tablespoons olive oil, divided
- 6 boneless, skinless chicken breasts
- 1 cup pomegranate juice (no sugar added)
- 2 tablespoons honey
- 1 tablespoon Dijon mustard
- 1/2 teaspoon dried thyme
- 1 fresh pomegranate, seeds removed

Mix the cumin, garlic, sea salt, and freshly ground pepper with 2 tablespoons of olive oil, and rub into the chicken.

Heat the remaining olive oil in a large skillet over medium heat.

Add the chicken breasts and sauté for 10 minutes, turning halfway through the cooking time, so the chicken breasts are golden brown on each side.

Add the pomegranate juice, honey, Dijon mustard, and thyme.

Lower the heat and simmer for 20 minutes, or until the chicken is cooked through and the sauce reduces by half.

Transfer the chicken and sauce to a serving platter, and top with fresh pomegranate seeds.

Serves 6.

Roast Chicken

Roast chicken may seem intimidating, but it's actually one of the simplest chicken dishes you can make. Remember, small portions of meat and large portions of vegetables are the Mediterranean way! Prepare this chicken for a lazy Sunday dinner, and you'll have leftovers for lunch on Monday.

- 1/4 cup white wine
- 2 tablespoons olive oil, divided
- 1 tablespoon Dijon mustard
- 1 garlic clove, minced
- 1 teaspoon dried rosemary
- Juice and zest of 1 lemon
- Sea salt and freshly ground pepper, to taste
- 1 large roasting chicken, giblets removed
- 3 large carrots, peeled and cut into chunks
- 1 fennel bulb, peeled and cut into 1/2-inch cubes
- 2 celery stalks, cut into chunks

Preheat the oven to 400 degrees.

Combine the white wine, 1 tablespoon of olive oil, mustard, garlic, rosemary, lemon juice and zest, sea salt, and freshly ground pepper in a small bowl.

Place the chicken in a shallow roasting pan on a roasting rack.

Rub the entire chicken, including the cavity, with the wine and mustard mixture.

Place the chicken in the oven and roast for 15 minutes.

Toss the vegetables with the remaining tablespoon of olive oil, and place around the chicken.

Turn the heat down to 375 degrees.

Roast an additional 40–60 minutes, basting the chicken every 15 minutes with the drippings in the bottom of the pan.

Cook chicken until internal temperature reaches 170–180 degrees in between the thigh and the body of the chicken. When you remove the instant-read thermometer, the juices should run clear.

Let the chicken rest for at least 10–15 minutes before serving.

Serves 4.

Roasted Cornish Hen with Figs

Tiny Cornish hens make an elegant presentation for any special dinner. The figs and white wine add sweetness and depth to this simple dish, while fresh figs provide a good source of fiber.

• 2 Cornish game hens	• Sea salt and freshly ground pepper, to taste
• 2 tablespoons olive oil	
• 1 tablespoon Herbes de Provence	• 1 pound fresh figs
	• 1 cup dry white wine

Preheat the oven to 350 degrees.

Place the Cornish hens in a shallow roasting pan and brush them with olive oil.

Season liberally with Herbes de Provence, sea salt, and freshly ground pepper.

Roast the hens for 15 minutes, or until golden brown.

Add the figs and white wine, and cover the hens with aluminum foil.

Cook an additional 20–30 minutes, or until the hens are cooked through.

Allow to rest for 10 minutes before serving.

Serves 2.

9

MEAT DISHES

- Afelia
- Albondigas (Spanish Meatballs)
- Beef and Polenta
- Beef and Wild Mushroom Stew
- Beef Stew
- Flank Steak and Blue Cheese Wraps
- Greek Kebabs
- Lamb and Vegetable Bake
- Lamb Couscous
- Lamb Stew
- Pork and Cannellini Bean Stew
- Pork Loin in Dried Fig Sauce
- Roast Pork Tenderloin
- Stuffed Flank Steak
- Zesty Grilled Flank Steak

Afelia

Afelia is a classic stew from Cyprus. It gets its unique flavor from coriander, cinnamon, and red wine. Serve it with brown rice or oven-roasted potatoes and a green salad. The following day, leftovers can be stuffed in a whole-wheat pita or wrap.

- 2 pounds boneless pork roast, cut into 2-inch pieces
- 1 cup red wine
- 1 tablespoon crushed coriander seeds
- 1 cinnamon stick
- Sea salt and freshly ground pepper, to taste
- 1/4 cup olive oil
- 1 cup small white onions, peeled
- 3 bay leaves

Place the pork chunks in a shallow bowl.

Add the red wine, coriander seeds, and cinnamon stick, and marinate for several hours or overnight.

Drain, reserving the liquid, and pat the pork chunks dry with a paper towel.

Season the pork with sea salt and freshly ground pepper.

Heat the olive oil in a large stew pot or skillet.

Add the pork and onions, and cook for 8–10 minutes, stirring frequently.

Add the bay leaves, sea salt, freshly ground pepper, and reserved liquid.

Cover and simmer on low for 2 hours, or until the pork is very tender.

Remove the lid, take out the bay leaves, simmer an additional 15 minutes to thicken the sauce, and serve.

Serves 6.

Albondigas (Spanish Meatballs)

This is a classic dish that you'll find in many restaurants and homes throughout Spain. Serve with rice, potatoes, or bread to mop up the beefy sauce. Use the leanest beef you can find to save on calories.

For the meatballs:
- 1 cup milk
- 2 slices stale bread
- 1/2 cup onion, minced
- 1/4 cup flat-leaf parsley, chopped
- 1 egg
- 1–2 cloves garlic, minced
- 1/2 teaspoon freshly ground pepper
- 1/2 teaspoon sea salt
- 1 pound ground beef
- 1 cup olive oil

For the sauce:
- 2 tablespoons olive oil
- 1/4 cup minced onion
- 1 clove garlic, minced
- 1 tablespoon flour
- 1 cup beef broth
- 1/4 cup red wine
- Pinch saffron threads
- 1/2 teaspoon hot paprika

Make the meatballs:

Combine the milk and bread, and soften 5–10 minutes. Squeeze out the excess milk from the bread.

Add the onion, parsley, egg, and garlic, and season with sea salt and freshly ground pepper.

Use your hands to mix the ground beef into the bread mixture, thoroughly combining.

Heat the olive oil in a large skillet.

Form the ground beef mixture into 1-inch balls, (roughly 30–40 meatballs) and fry in the oil until completely cooked and lightly browned.

Transfer to a paper towel to drain.

Make the sauce:

In a saucepan, heat the olive oil.

Sauté the onion and garlic until softened.

Whisk in the flour, stirring constantly for 30 seconds.

Whisk in the beef broth and wine, and simmer until thickened slightly.

Stir in the saffron and hot paprika.

Pour the sauce over the meatballs to serve.

Serves 4.

Beef and Polenta

Italian polenta makes a wonderful accompaniment to rich stews, and can take the place of mashed potatoes or noodles. Serve this Italian-style stew with a hearty vegetable side dish.

- 1/4 cup olive oil
- 2 pounds lean, boneless beef, cut into 2-inch cubes
- 1 yellow onion, peeled and chopped
- 3 cloves garlic, minced
- 1 cup white wine
- 1 (10-ounce) can tomato sauce
- 1 teaspoon dried rosemary
- 1 bay leaf
- 1/2 teaspoon chipotle chili powder or red chili powder
- 1 package prepared polenta

Heat the olive oil in a large stew pot over medium-high heat.

Add the beef and cook 10–12 minutes, stirring occasionally to brown on all sides.

Add the onion and garlic, and cook an additional 5 minutes, or until the onion is tender.

Deglaze the bottom of the pot with the wine, making sure to scrape up the brown bits with a wooden spoon.

Stir in the tomato sauce, herbs, and chili powder.

Cover and simmer for up to 2 hours, or until the beef is very tender.

Prepare the polenta according to package directions.

Remove the bay leaf, and serve the beef stew with the polenta.

Serves 4.

Beef and Wild Mushroom Stew

Earthy, rich, and full of flavor, this stew is an excellent choice for a simple meal. Serve it with a green salad, vegetable side dish, and whole-wheat bread. For a thriftier option than pricey porcini or morels, substitute oyster or portobello mushrooms.

- 2 pounds fresh porcini or morel mushrooms
- 1/3 cup olive oil
- 2 pounds lean, boneless beef, cut into 2-inch cubes
- 2 medium onions, finely chopped
- 1 clove garlic, minced
- 1 cup dry white wine
- 1 teaspoon thyme, minced
- Sea salt and freshly ground pepper, to taste

Wash the mushrooms carefully by soaking them in cold water and swirling them around.

Trim away any soft parts of the mushrooms.

Heat the olive oil in a heavy stew pot over medium-high heat.

Brown the meat evenly on all sides, and set aside on a plate.

Add the onions, garlic, and mushrooms to the olive oil, and cook for 5–8 minutes, or until the onions are tender, stirring frequently.

Add the remaining ingredients and return the browned meat to the pot.

Cover and bring to a boil, then reduce heat to low and simmer.

Simmer for 1 hour, or until the meat is tender and flavorful.

Season with sea salt and freshly ground pepper to taste.

Serves 8.

Beef Stew

This humble beef stew gets its rich flavor from a red wine marinade, and tastes even better if prepared a day ahead. Serve it with whole-wheat noodles or brown rice.

For the marinade:
- 1 cup red wine
- 1/2 cup olive oil
- 1 medium onion, sliced
- 1 celery stalk, sliced
- 1/4 cup brandy
- 2 cloves garlic, minced
- 3/4 teaspoon dried thyme
- Zest of 1 orange

For the stew:
- 2 pounds lean beef stew or pot roast, cut into 2-inch cubes
- 2 tablespoons olive oil
- Sea salt and freshly ground pepper, to taste
- 1 tablespoon instant flour
- 6 medium carrots, peeled and cut into 1-inch slices
- 14 small pearl onions, peeled
- 1 (14-ounce) can chopped tomatoes, drained
- 1 cup low-salt olives, pitted

Make the marinade:

Combine the marinade ingredients in a plastic bag and add beef.

Shake well to coat, and refrigerate for up to 24 hours.

Drain and discard the marinade.

Make the stew:

In a heavy stew pot, heat the olive oil over medium-high heat.

Season the meat with sea salt and freshly ground pepper, and toss with flour.

Brown the meat in the oil for 8–10 minutes, stirring frequently until all sides are well browned.

Add the remaining ingredients.

Simmer on low for up to 2 hours, or until the carrots and meat are tender.

Serve stew on a bed of noodles or rice.

Serves 8.

Flank Steak and Blue Cheese Wraps

This snack or lunch dish uses leftover flank steak. Heat the flank steak if you like, or serve it cold. To boost the nutrition of these wraps, add fresh spinach leaves.

- 1 cup leftover flank steak, cut into 1-inch slices
- 1/4 cup red onion, thinly sliced
- 1/4 cup cherry tomatoes, chopped
- 1/4 cup low-salt olives, pitted and chopped
- 1/4 cup roasted red bell peppers, drained and coarsely chopped
- 1/4 cup blue cheese crumbles
- 6 whole-wheat or spinach wraps
- Sea salt and freshly ground pepper, to taste

Combine the flank steak, onion, tomatoes, olives, bell pepper, and blue cheese in a small bowl.

Spread 1/2 cup of this mixture on each wrap, and roll halfway. Fold the end in, and finish rolling like a burrito.

Cut on a diagonal if you'd like, season to taste, and serve.

Serves 6.

Greek Kebabs

Olive oil, lemon, oregano, garlic, and bay leaves are classic Greek seasonings. Lean meat like sirloin beef is a good source of protein you can enjoy a few times a week on this diet. Serve kebabs with grilled vegetables.

- 1/4 cup olive oil
- Juice of 1 lemon
- 1 tablespoon dried oregano
- 2 cloves garlic, minced
- 5 bay leaves
- Sea salt and freshly ground pepper, to taste
- 2 pounds beef sirloin, cut into 2-inch cubes

Combine all the ingredients except the meat in a plastic bag. Add the meat and shake to coat.

Marinate for up to 24 hours and drain.

Skewer the meat onto 8-inch skewers and grill on medium heat for 8–10 minutes, turning the skewers halfway through the cooking time.

Serves 6.

Lamb and Vegetable Bake

This Greek-inspired one-dish meal combines lamb with a variety of garden vegetables. Improvise with the vegetables available in your garden or at your local farmers' market, but to maintain the authentic flavor, don't change the seasonings.

- 1/4 cup olive oil
- 1 pound boneless, lean lamb, cut into 1/2-inch pieces
- 2 large red potatoes, scrubbed and diced
- 1 large onion, coarsely chopped
- 2 cloves garlic, minced
- 1 (28-ounce) can diced tomatoes with liquid (no salt added)
- 2 medium zucchini, cut into 1/2-inch slices
- 1 red bell pepper, seeded and cut into 1-inch cubes
- 2 tablespoons flat-leaf parsley, chopped
- 1 teaspoon dried thyme
- 1 tablespoon paprika
- 1/2 teaspoon ground cinnamon
- 1/2 cup red wine
- Sea salt and freshly ground pepper, to taste

Preheat the oven to 325 degrees.

Heat the olive oil in a large stew pot or cast-iron skillet over medium-high heat.

Add the lamb and brown the meat, stirring frequently.

Transfer the lamb to an ovenproof baking dish.

Cook the potatoes, onion, and garlic in the skillet until tender, then transfer them to the baking dish.

Pour the tomatoes, zucchini, and pepper into the pan along with the herbs and spices, and simmer for 10 minutes.

Cover the lamb, onions, and potatoes with the tomato and pepper sauce and wine.

Cover with aluminum foil and bake for 1 hour. Uncover during the last 15 minutes of baking.

Season to taste, and serve with a green salad.

Serves 8.

Lamb Couscous

Choose a whole-wheat couscous for a more nutritious dish, and steam the couscous instead of boiling it for fewer calories. Since this dish serves so many, it's a great choice for parties.

- 2 pounds boneless lamb meat, cut into 2-inch pieces
- 1/2 teaspoon dried thyme
- 1/2 teaspoon dried marjoram
- Sea salt and freshly ground pepper, to taste
- 1/4 cup olive oil
- 1 onion, peeled and coarsely chopped
- 1 bulb celeriac, cut in chunks
- 5 cups chicken broth
- 2 zucchini, cut into 1-inch pieces
- 1 cup cooked chickpeas
- 1 cup raisins (optional)
- 1/4 teaspoon ground ginger
- 1/4 teaspoon ground cinnamon
- 1/4 teaspoon ground cardamom
- 1/4 teaspoon ground cloves
- 1/4 teaspoon ground nutmeg
- 5 cups cooked whole-wheat couscous
- 1/2 cup fresh cilantro, chopped
- 1/2 cup fresh mint, chopped
- 1/4 cup green onions, chopped

Season the lamb meat with the thyme, marjoram, sea salt, and freshly ground pepper, and grill in a grill basket for 8–10 minutes, stirring frequently.

If you don't have a grill basket, you can also cook the lamb in a heavy skillet.

Set aside, but keep warm.

Heat the olive oil in a large skillet.

Add the onion and celeriac, and cook until tender, stirring frequently.

Add the chicken broth, zucchini, chickpeas, raisins, and spices, and simmer 10–20 minutes.

To serve, mound the couscous in the middle of a serving platter and arrange the vegetables and meat around the couscous. Garnish with the fresh cilantro, mint, and green onions.

Serves 8–10.

Lamb Stew

This lamb stew is seasoned with Provençal seasonings for a taste of France. Perfect for a light, spring meal, lamb stew tastes even better the next day. Serve with a vegetable salad and a whole-wheat baguette.

- 3 carrots, peeled and sliced
- 2 onions, minced
- 2 cups white wine
- 1/2 cup flat-leaf parsley, chopped
- 2 garlic cloves, minced
- 3 bay leaves
- 1 teaspoon dried rosemary leaves
- 1/4 teaspoon nutmeg
- 1/4 teaspoon ground cloves
- 2 pounds boneless lamb, cut into 1-inch pieces
- 1/4 cup olive oil
- 1 package frozen artichoke hearts
- Sea salt and freshly ground pepper, to taste

Combine the carrots, onion, white wine, parsley, garlic, bay leaves, and seasonings in a plastic bag or shallow dish.

Add the lamb and marinate overnight.

Drain the lamb, reserving the marinade, and pat dry.

Heat the olive oil in a large stew pot. Brown the lamb meat, turning frequently.

Pour the marinade into the stew pot, cover, and simmer on low for 2 hours.

Add the artichoke hearts and simmer an additional 20 minutes.

Season with sea salt and freshly ground pepper.

Serves 6.

Pork and Cannellini Bean Stew

This delectable Greek stew is the ultimate budget dish. Hearty and filling, it costs surprisingly little per serving. Serve with a salad and two vegetable side dishes for a full meal.

- 1 cup dried cannellini beans
- 1/4 cup olive oil
- 1 medium onion, diced
- 2 pounds pork roast, cut into 1-inch chunks
- 3 cups water
- 1 (8-ounce) can tomato paste
- 1/4 cup flat-leaf parsley, chopped
- 1/2 teaspoon dried thyme
- Sea salt and freshly ground pepper, to taste

Rinse and sort the beans.

Cover beans with water, and allow to soak overnight.

Heat the olive oil in a large stew pot.

Add the onion, stirring occasionally, until golden brown.

Add the pork chunks and cook 5–8 minutes, stirring frequently, until the pork is browned. Drain and rinse the beans, and add to the pot.

Add the water, and bring to a boil. Reduce heat and simmer for 45 minutes, until beans are tender.

Add the tomato paste, parsley, and thyme, and simmer an additional 15 minutes, or until the sauce thickens slightly. Season to taste.

Serves 6.

Pork Loin in Dried Fig Sauce

Pork loin is a lean meat and pairs beautifully with fruit or fruity wine. If you can't find dried figs, substitute apricots instead. Both dried figs and apricots are high in fiber.

- 3 teaspoon fresh rosemary
- 1 tablespoon fresh thyme
- Sea salt and freshly ground pepper, to taste
- 1 (3-pound) pork loin
- 1/2 cup olive oil
- 3 carrots, peeled and sliced
- 1 onion, diced
- 1 garlic clove, minced
- 1 cup dried figs, cut into small pieces
- 1 cup white wine
- Juice of 1 lemon

Preheat the oven to 300 degrees.

Mix the rosemary, thyme, sea salt, and freshly ground pepper together to make a dry rub. Press the rub into the pork loin.

Heat the olive oil in a skillet.

Add the pork loin, carrots, onion, and garlic, and cook for 15 minutes, or until the pork is browned.

Transfer all to a shallow roasting pan.

Add the figs, white wine, and lemon juice.

Cover with aluminum foil and bake for 40–50 minutes, or until the meat is tender and internal temperature is about 145 degrees.

Transfer the meat to a serving dish, and cover with aluminum foil.

Wait 15 minutes before slicing.

In the meantime, pour the vegetables, figs, and liquids into a blender. Process until smooth and strain through a sieve or strainer.

Transfer to a gravy dish, or pour directly over the sliced meat.

Serves 6.

Roast Pork Tenderloin

By simply altering the seasonings slightly, this traditional pork tenderloin takes on a decidedly Spanish flair. Remember, the diet allows red meat once per week. Serve it with red potatoes, or add it to salads, wraps, or sandwiches.

- 2 tablespoons olive oil
- 1 teaspoon Spanish paprika
- 1 teaspoon red wine vinegar
- 1 clove garlic, minced
- 1/2 teaspoon ground cumin
- 1/2 teaspoon ground coriander
- 1/2 teaspoon ginger
- 1/2 teaspoon freshly ground pepper
- 1/4 teaspoon turmeric
- 1 pound pork tenderloin
- Sea salt and freshly ground pepper, to taste

Combine all the ingredients except the pork tenderloin.

Spread over the meat in a thick paste, cover, and refrigerate for several hours or overnight.

Heat a grill to medium heat, and grill the tenderloin for 10–12 minutes, turning halfway through. An instant-read thermometer should read 145 degrees.

Transfer the meat to a serving platter, and allow it to rest for 15 minutes before slicing.

Season to taste and serve.

Serves 6.

Stuffed Flank Steak

In this dish, flank steak becomes tender through slow cooking, making it the perfect dish for a busy day. Simply prepare it the night before, turn the slow cooker on in the morning, and dinner is ready when you are. Almonds, tomatoes, spinach, and red peppers give this both a nutritional boost and a Mediterranean flavor.

- 2 pounds flank steak
- Sea salt and freshly ground pepper, to taste
- 1 tablespoon olive oil
- 1/4 cup onion, diced
- 1 clove garlic, minced
- 2 cups baby spinach, chopped
- 1/2 cup dried tomatoes, chopped
- 1/2 cup roasted red peppers, diced
- 1/2 cup almonds, toasted and chopped
- Kitchen twine
- 1/2 cup chicken stock

Lay the flank steak out on a cutting board, and generously season with sea salt and freshly ground pepper

Heat the olive oil in a medium saucepan.

Add the onion and garlic.

Cook 5 minutes on medium heat, or until onion is tender and translucent, stirring frequently.

Add the spinach, tomatoes, peppers, and chopped almonds, and cook an additional 3 minutes, or until the spinach wilts slightly.

Let the tomato and spinach mixture cool to room temperature.

Spread the tomato and spinach mixture evenly over the flank steak.

Roll the flank steak up slowly, and tie it securely with kitchen twine on both ends and in the middle.

Brown the flank steak in the same pan for 5 minutes, turning it carefully to brown all sides.

Place steak in a slow cooker with the chicken stock. Cover and cook on low for 4–6 hours.

Cut into rounds, discarding the twine, and serve.

Serves 6.

Zesty Grilled Flank Steak

Flank steak is a lean cut of meat that benefits from a long, slow marinade. Start marinating the meat the night before, and you're ready to go. Thin slices of lean steak can be served over a salad or pile of fresh vegetables. Make sure you are always eating a larger portion of vegetables than meat at any meal.

- 1/4 cup olive oil
- 3 tablespoons red wine vinegar
- 1 teaspoon dried rosemary
- 1 teaspoon dried marjoram
- 1 teaspoon dried oregano

- 1 teaspoon paprika
- 2 cloves garlic, minced
- 1 teaspoon freshly ground pepper
- 2 pounds flank steak

Combine the olive oil, vinegar, herbs, and seasonings in a small bowl.

Place the flank steak in a shallow dish, and rub the marinade into the meat.

Cover and refrigerate for up to 24 hours.

Heat a charcoal or gas grill to medium heat (350–375 degrees).

Grill the steak for 18–21 minutes, turning once halfway through the cooking time.

An internal meat thermometer should read 135–140 degrees when the meat is done.

Transfer the meat to a cutting board, and cover with aluminum foil. Let steak rest for at least 10 minutes.

Slice against the grain very thinly and serve.

Serves 6.

(10)

SEAFOOD DISHES

- Almond-Encrusted Salmon
- Baked Salmon with Capers and Olives
- Balsamic-Glazed Black Pepper Salmon
- Bouillabaisse
- Burgundy Salmon
- Chermoula Salmon
- Clam Spaghetti
- Cod Gratin
- Grilled Bluefish
- Grilled Herbed Tuna
- Halibut with Roasted Vegetables
- Herb-Marinated Flounder
- Poached Cod
- Roasted Sea Bass
- Shrimp Salad

Almond-Encrusted Salmon

Crushed almonds give this salmon a sweet and savory crunch. Salmon and almonds are both a good source of healthful fats. Make enough to use the leftovers in a green salad.

- 1/4 cup olive oil
- 1 tablespoon honey
- 1/4 cup breadcrumbs
- 1/2 cup finely chopped almonds, lightly toasted

- 1/2 teaspoon dried thyme
- Sea salt and freshly ground pepper, to taste
- 4 salmon steaks

Preheat the oven to 350 degrees.

Combine the olive oil with the honey. (Soften the honey in the microwave for 15 seconds, if necessary, for easier blending.)

In a shallow dish, combine the breadcrumbs, almonds, thyme, sea salt, and freshly ground pepper.

Coat the salmon steaks with the olive oil mixture, then the almond mixture.

Place on a baking sheet brushed with olive oil and bake 8–12 minutes, or until the almonds are lightly browned and the salmon is firm.

Serves 4.

Baked Salmon with Capers and Olives

This fresh-tasting salmon dish is inspired by the cuisine of Greece and Italy. Salmon is a great source of omega-3 fatty acids.

- 1 tablespoon olive oil, divided
- 4 salmon steaks
- Sea salt and freshly ground pepper, to taste
- 2 Roma tomatoes, chopped
- 1/4 cup green olives, pitted and chopped
- 1 clove garlic, minced
- Juice of 1/2 lemon
- 1 teaspoon capers, rinsed and drained
- 1/2 teaspoon sugar
- 1/2 cup dry breadcrumbs

Preheat the oven to 375 degrees.

Brush a baking dish with the olive oil. Place the salmon fillets in the dish.

Season with sea salt and freshly ground pepper.

In a large bowl, combine all the remaining ingredients.

Top the salmon fillets with the tomato mixture, then the breadcrumbs.

Drizzle with the remaining olive oil and bake for 15 minutes, or until medium rare.

Serves 4.

Balsamic-Glazed Black Pepper Salmon

Salmon is a rich and fatty fish that is high in health benefits. When purchasing the fish, choose wild Pacific salmon whenever possible. This particular dish pairs well with a light Pinot Noir.

- 1/2 cup balsamic vinegar
- 1 tablespoon honey
- 4 (8-ounce) salmon filets
- Sea salt and freshly ground pepper, to taste
- 1 tablespoon olive oil

Heat a cast-iron skillet over medium-high heat.

Mix the vinegar and honey in a small bowl.

Season the salmon filets with the sea salt and freshly ground pepper; brush with the honey-balsamic glaze.

Add olive oil to the skillet, and sear the salmon filets, cooking for 3–4 minutes on each side until lightly browned and medium rare in the center.

Let sit for 5 minutes before serving.

Serves 4.

Bouillabaisse

Bouillabaisse is an aromatic soup from Marseilles. Seafood can be enjoyed a several times a week on the Mediterranean diet. Classic recipes call for a variety of seafood, so feel free to use what you can find, and don't worry—the results will still be delicious. Serve over brown rice with a large green salad.

- 1/2 cup olive oil
- 2 onions, diced
- 4 tomatoes, peeled and chopped
- 5 cloves garlic, minced
- 3 pints low-salt fish stock
- 8 small red potatoes, cubed and cooked
- 1 cup white wine
- 1 bunch basil leaves, finely chopped
- 1 tablespoon Tabasco or other hot sauce
- 1 teaspoon dried thyme
- 1/2 teaspoon saffron
- 10 clams, scrubbed
- 10 mussels, scrubbed
- 1 pound shrimp, peeled, deveined, and tails removed
- 1 pound fresh monkfish fillets, cut into chunks
- 1 pound fresh cod, cut into chunks
- 1/2 cup flat-leaf parsley, chopped

Heat the olive oil in a large stockpot over medium-high heat.

Add the onions and cook for 5 minutes, or until the onions are soft and translucent.

Add the tomatoes and garlic, and simmer 5 minutes more.

Add the fish stock, potatoes, wine, basil, hot sauce, thyme, and saffron, and simmer for 20 minutes.

Puree half of this mixture in the blender, then return to stockpot.

Add the shellfish, shrimp, fish, and parsley, and simmer 20 minutes.

Serve with brown rice.

Serves 8.

Burgundy Salmon

Red wine is usually associated with beef, but here it complements rich salmon. Wild salmon is a healthier choice for you and the environment than farmed Atlantic salmon. Serve this dish with plenty of fresh green vegetables and potatoes.

- 4 salmon steaks
- Sea salt and freshly ground pepper, to taste
- 1 tablespoon olive oil
- 1 shallot, minced
- 2 cups high-quality Burgundy wine
- 1/2 cup beef stock
- 2 tablespoons tomato paste
- 1 teaspoon fresh thyme, chopped

Preheat the oven to 350 degrees.

Season the salmon steaks with sea salt and freshly ground pepper. Wrap the salmon steaks in aluminum foil and bake for 10–13 minutes.

Heat the olive oil in a deep skillet on medium heat. Add the shallot and cook for 3 minutes, or until tender.

Add the wine, beef stock, and tomato paste, and simmer for 10 minutes, or until sauce thickens and reduces by 1/3.

Place the fish on a serving platter and spoon the sauce over it.

Sprinkle the fish with the fresh thyme, and serve.

Serves 4.

Chermoula Salmon

Chermoula is a traditional Moroccan marinade that is typically used with fish. Ingredients include cilantro, a good source of phytonutrients, and parsley, which provides high levels of vitamin K. The marinade keeps for up to a week in the refrigerator.

- 1/2 cup olive oil
- 1/2 cup fresh cilantro, chopped
- 1/2 cup flat-leaf parsley, chopped
- 4 garlic cloves, minced
- Juice of 1 lemon
- 1 tablespoon cumin
- 1 tablespoon dried red chili pepper
- 1 tablespoon paprika
- 1 teaspoon sea salt
- 4 salmon filets

Preheat the oven to 450 degrees.

Combine all the ingredients except the salmon in a small saucepan.

Heat over medium heat just until the mixture is hot, but do not let it boil. Then let cool to room temperature.

Place the salmon on a baking sheet, and rub the marinade over it.

Cover and refrigerate for up to 4 hours.

Bake for 10–13 minutes, or until the salmon is cooked medium rare and is slightly firm to the touch.

Serves 4.

Clam Spaghetti

Nothing could be simpler for a weeknight meal than this easy pasta dish. Clams are rich in iron, protein, omega-3 fatty acids, and vitamin B12. Leave out the bacon if you are trying to cut calories.

- 1/4 cup olive oil
- 4 ounces bacon
- 1 medium onion, diced
- 1 medium green pepper, seeded and diced
- 4 garlic cloves, minced
- 1/2 cup flat-leaf parsley, chopped
- 1/3 teaspoon cayenne pepper
- Sea salt and freshly ground pepper, to taste
- 3 dozen or so clams, depending on their size
- 1/2 cup white wine
- 1 pound whole-wheat spaghetti
- 1 lemon, cut into wedges
- 1/2 cup freshly grated, low-fat Parmesan cheese

Heat the olive oil in a large skillet over medium heat.

Add the bacon, onion, pepper, and garlic, and cook until the bacon is slightly crisp and the onion is translucent.

Add the parsley, cayenne pepper, sea salt, and freshly ground pepper, and set aside.

Bring a pot of water to a boil.

Add the clams and boil for 10 minutes, or until they open. Remove the clams from the pot, and shell half of them.

Return the skillet to medium-high heat.

Add the shelled clams to the skillet, along with the remaining clams, white wine, and 2 cups of the liquid used to boil the clams.

Cook the pasta according to package directions for al dente, and place in a large serving dish.

Ladle the clam and bacon mixture over the pasta, and toss to serve.

Garnish with lemon wedges and Parmesan cheese.

Serves 4.

Cod Gratin

A gratin is any dish with a crispy topping of breadcrumbs or cheese. In this tasty French-inspired dish, cod, leeks, and onion peek out from a whole-wheat breadcrumb crust. Serve with sautéed greens, such as spinach, chard, or kale.

- 1/2 cup olive oil, divided
- 1 pound fresh cod
- 1 cup black olives, pitted and chopped
- 4 leeks, trimmed and sliced
- 1 cup whole-wheat breadcrumbs
- 3/4 cup low-salt chicken stock
- Sea salt and freshly ground pepper, to taste

Preheat the oven to 350 degrees.

Brush 4 gratin dishes with the olive oil.

Place the cod on a baking dish, and bake for 5–7 minutes.

Cool and cut into 1-inch pieces.

Heat the remaining olive oil in a large skillet.

Add the olives and leeks, and cook over medium-low heat until the leeks are tender.

Add the breadcrumbs and chicken stock, stirring to mix.

Gently fold in the pieces of cod. Divide the mixture between the 4 gratin dishes, and drizzle with olive oil.

Season with sea salt and freshly ground pepper.

Bake for 15 minutes or until warmed through.

Serves 4.

Grilled Bluefish

The citrus in this dish lends it a sunny Mediterranean flavor. If you can find small, whole bluefish, clean and grill them whole. Otherwise, filets work fine. Bluefish is a good source of niacin, phosphorus, selenium, and vitamin B6 and B12.

- 1 cup olive oil
- 1/2 cup white wine
- 1/4 cup fresh basil leaves, chopped
- Juice and zest of 2 lemons or oranges
- 2–3 garlic cloves, minced
- 1 teaspoon ground cumin
- 1 teaspoon thyme
- 2 pinches cayenne pepper
- 4 bluefish or fish filets
- Sea salt and freshly ground pepper, to taste

Combine all the ingredients except the fish in a plastic bag or shallow bowl.

Divide marinade in half, reserving half in the refrigerator and placing the fish in the other half of the marinade.

Refrigerate for at least 1 hour.

Heat the grill to medium-high.

Brush the grates with olive oil, and grill the fish for 6–8 minutes, turning halfway through the cooking time.

Season with sea salt and freshly ground pepper, to taste.

Warm the reserved marinade and serve with the fish.

Serves 4.

Grilled Herbed Tuna

Tuna is a meaty fish that stands up well to grilling. Just be sure to brush the grill grates with oil before adding the fish so it doesn't stick.

- 2 tablespoons olive oil
- 2 tablespoons fresh basil, chopped
- Juice and zest of 1 lemon
- 2 teaspoons fresh cilantro, chopped
- 1 clove garlic, minced
- Sea salt and freshly ground pepper, to taste
- 4 fresh tuna steaks
- 2 tablespoons flat-leaf parsley, chopped

Preheat the grill to medium-high.

Combine all the ingredients except the fish and parsley in a bowl.

Brush each side of the tuna with the herb mixture, and let marinate for at least 30 minutes in the refrigerator.

Grill 8–12 minutes depending on thickness, turning halfway through the cooking time.

Garnish with chopped parsley, season to taste, and serve immediately.

Serves 4.

Halibut with Roasted Vegetables

Halibut is a firm, mild fish that pairs well with a variety of seasonings and vegetables. Here, it's combined with tomatoes and zucchini—traditional Mediterranean vegetables—but feel free to improvise with what's available in your garden or farmers' market.

- 1/4 cup small white mushrooms, coarsely chopped
- 2 small tomatoes, coarsely chopped
- 1 small white onion, chopped
- 2 zucchini, chopped
- 2 cloves garlic, minced
- 1 teaspoon Herbes de Provence
- 1/2 cup olive oil
- Sea salt and freshly ground pepper, to taste
- 1 1/2 pounds halibut steak, cut into 6 pieces
- 3 tablespoons fresh tarragon, chopped finely
- Juice of 1 lemon

Preheat the oven to 350 degrees.

Toss the vegetables and herbs on a large baking sheet with the olive oil, and season with sea salt and freshly ground pepper.

Roast for 15–20 minutes, or until soft and slightly browned. Do not burn.

Place the halibut steaks on another baking sheet, and season with the tarragon, sea salt, freshly ground pepper, and lemon juice.

Roast for 10–13 minutes.

Top the halibut steaks with the roasted vegetables.

Serves 6.

Herb-Marinated Flounder

Although dried herbs work in many recipes, fresh herbs are much tastier. Fresh herbs are also a better source of antioxidants than dry herbs. Most herbs grow easily in a pot on your back step, or even a sunny windowsill in your kitchen.

- 1/2 cup lightly packed flat-leaf parsley
- 1/4 cup olive oil
- 4 garlic cloves, peeled and halved
- 2 tablespoons fresh rosemary
- 2 tablespoons fresh thyme leaves
- 2 tablespoons fresh sage
- 2 tablespoons lemon zest
- Sea salt and freshly ground pepper, to taste
- 4 flounder filets

Preheat the oven to 350 degrees.

Place all the ingredients except the fish in a food processor.

Blend to form a thick paste.

Place the filets on a baking sheet, and brush this paste on them. Refrigerate for at least 1 hour.

Bake for 8–10 minutes, or until the flounder is slightly firm and opaque.

Season with sea salt and freshly ground pepper.

Serves 4.

Poached Cod

Poaching is an ideal method for cooking soft fish, such as cod. Although this recipe calls for cod, substitute any white fish.

- 1 tablespoon olive oil
- 1/2 cup onion, thinly sliced
- 1 cup fennel, thinly sliced
- 1 tablespoon garlic, minced
- 1 (15-ounce) can diced tomatoes
- 2 cups chicken broth
- 1/2 cup white wine
- Juice and zest of 1 orange
- 1 pinch red pepper flakes
- 1 bay leaf
- 1 pound cod

Heat the olive oil in a large skillet. Add the onion and fennel, and cook 10 minutes, or until translucent and soft.

Add the garlic and cook 1 minute.

Add the tomatoes, chicken broth, wine, orange juice and zest, red pepper flakes, and bay leaf, and simmer for 5 minutes to meld the flavors.

Carefully add the fish in a single layer.

Cover and simmer 6–7 minutes.

Transfer fish to a serving dish, Ladle the remaining sauce over the fish.

Serves 4.

Roasted Sea Bass

Roasting is an easy and forgiving way to prepare almost any fish. Use it to cook whole fish, fish filets, or even fish chunks, and simply adjust the cooking time based on the fish's size. Enjoy this dish with sautéed greens and potatoes.

- 1/4 cup olive oil
- Whole sea bass or filets
- Sea salt and freshly ground pepper, to taste
- 1/4 cup dry white wine
- 3 teaspoons fresh dill
- 2 teaspoons fresh thyme
- 1 garlic clove, minced

Preheat the oven to 425 degrees.

Brush the bottom of a roasting pan with olive oil. Place the fish in the pan and brush the fish with oil.

Season fish with sea salt and freshly ground pepper.

Combine the remaining ingredients and pour over the fish.

Bake for 10–15 minutes, depending on the size of the fish.

Sea bass is done when the flesh is firm and opaque.

Serves 6.

Shrimp Salad

Main dish salads are a great way to get many servings of vegetables in one meal. Serve this tasty fare with whole-wheat pita bread for a light lunch or dinner.

For the vinaigrette:
- 1/8 cup red wine vinegar
- Juice of 1 lemon
- 1 small shallot, finely minced
- 1 tablespoon fresh mint, chopped
- 1/4 teaspoon dried oregano
- 1/4 cup olive oil
- Sea salt and freshly ground pepper, to taste

For the salad:
- 1 pound shrimp, deveined and shelled
- Juice and zest of 1 lemon
- 1 clove garlic, minced
- 2 cups baby spinach leaves
- 1 cup romaine lettuce, chopped
- 1/2 cup grape tomatoes
- 1 medium cucumber, peeled, seeded, and diced
- 1/2 cup low-salt olives, pitted
- 1/4 cup low-fat feta cheese

Make the vinaigrette:

Combine the wine vinegar, lemon juice, shallot, chopped mint, and oregano in a bowl.

Add the olive oil, whisking constantly for up to 1 minute, or until you create a smooth emulsion, then season with sea salt and freshly ground pepper.

Refrigerate for 1 hour and whisk before serving if separated.

Make the salad:

Combine the shrimp with the lemon juice and garlic in a shallow bowl or bag. Marinate for at least 2 hours.

Grill the shrimp in a grill basket or sauté in a frying pan 2–3 minutes until pink.

In a large bowl, toss the greens, tomatoes, cucumber, olives, and feta cheese together.

Toss the shrimp with the salad mixture, and drizzle with the vinaigrette.

Serve immediately.

Serves 4.

VEGETABLE DISHES

- Braised Eggplant and Tomatoes
- Caramelized Root Vegetables
- Grilled Eggplant Pesto Stack
- Grilled Vegetables
- Mushroom-Stuffed Zucchini
- Roasted Balsamic Brussels Sprouts with Pecans
- Roasted Beets with Oranges and Onions
- Rosemary-Roasted Acorn Squash
- Sautéed Crunchy Greens
- Sautéed Mustard Greens and Red Peppers
- Stuffed Bell Peppers
- Stuffed Cucumbers
- Swiss Chard with White Beans and Bell Peppers
- Vibrant Green Beans

Braised Eggplant and Tomatoes

Eggplant and tomatoes are classic companions in Greek, Italian, and French foods. This thick vegetarian ragù is delicious enough to eat over crusty bread, grain, or pasta. Getting your daily allowance of vegetables is easy with a dish like this.

- 1 large eggplant, peeled and diced
- Pinch sea salt
- 1 (15-ounce) can chopped tomatoes and juices
- 1 cup chicken broth
- 2 garlic cloves, smashed
- 1 tablespoon Italian seasoning
- 1 bay leaf
- Sea salt and freshly ground pepper, to taste

Cut the eggplant, and salt both sides to remove bitter juices. Let the eggplant sit for 20 minutes before rinsing and patting dry.

Dice eggplant.

Put eggplant, tomatoes, chicken broth, garlic, seasoning, and bay leaf in a large saucepot.

Bring to a boil and reduce heat to simmer.

Cover and simmer for about 30–40 minutes until eggplant is tender.

Remove garlic cloves and bay leaf, season to taste, and serve.

Serves 4.

Caramelized Root Vegetables

Cooking the vegetables in this recipe slowly will allow them to develop color and sweetness without burning. Don't skip the seasonings—spices have nutrients and antioxidant power.

- 2 medium carrots, peeled and cut into chunks
- 2 medium red or gold beets, cut into chunks
- 2 turnips, peeled and cut into chunks
- 2 tablespoons olive oil
- 1 teaspoon cumin
- 1 teaspoon sweet paprika
- Sea salt and freshly ground pepper, to taste
- Juice of 1 lemon
- 1 small bunch flat-leaf parsley, chopped

Preheat oven to 400 degrees.

Toss the vegetables with the olive oil and seasonings.

Lay in a single layer on a sheet pan, cover with lemon juice, and roast for 30–40 minutes, until veggies are slightly browned and crisp.

Serve warm, topped with the chopped parsley.

Serves 6.

Grilled Eggplant Pesto Stack

This pretty stack is inspired by the flavors of Italy. Making pesto is a cinch, although the store-bought variety will work if you're looking to make this dish fast. Eggplant is hearty enough to be a great meat substitute.

For the pesto:
- 1 large bunch basil, or 1 cup tightly packed basil leaves
- 1/2 cup pine nuts, toasted
- 2–3 cloves garlic
- Juice of 1 lime
- 3/4 cup olive oil
- 1/2 cup freshly grated, low-fat Parmesan cheese
- Sea salt and freshly ground pepper, to taste

For the eggplant:
- 1 medium eggplant, sliced into 1/2-inch thick slices
- 2 tablespoons olive oil

Make the pesto:

Put the basil, pine nuts, garlic, and lime juice in a food processor, and pulse until a thick paste.

Continue to pulse and slowly drizzle in the olive oil until creamy.

Fold in the cheese unless you plan to freeze the pesto.

Season with sea salt and freshly ground pepper.

Make the eggplant:

Preheat a grill to medium-high heat.

Salt the eggplant and let rest for 20 minutes to get the bitter juices out.

Rinse the eggplant and pat dry with a paper towel.

Brush the eggplant with 2 tablespoons olive oil, and lay on the grill.

Grill for 5–6 minutes per side, until the eggplant is lightly charred but still firm.

To serve, layer the grilled eggplant with the pesto on individual plates.

Serves 4.

Grilled Vegetables

Grilling vegetables instead of burgers or steaks is a great way to enjoy that smoky barbecue flavor without all the fat and calories. Eating as well as cooking outdoors—dining alfresco—adds to the enjoyment of your meal, a key component of the diet. As this dish proves, less fat doesn't have to mean less flavor. Here, balsamic vinegar adds pizzazz to a variety of grilled vegetables. Feel free to substitute vegetables.

• 4 carrots, peeled and cut in half	• 1/4 cup olive oil
• 2 onions, quartered	• Sea salt and freshly ground pepper, to taste
• 1 zucchini, cut into 1/2-inch rounds	• Balsamic vinegar
• 1 red bell pepper, seeded and cut into cubes	

Heat the grill to medium-high.

Brush the vegetables lightly with olive oil, and season with sea salt and freshly ground pepper.

Place the carrots and onions on the grill first because they take the longest.

Cook the vegetables for 3–4 minutes on each side.

Transfer to a serving dish, and drizzle with olive oil and balsamic vinegar.

Serves 4.

Mushroom-Stuffed Zucchini

Fresh zucchini and mushrooms seasoned with garlic, olive oil, parsley, and Italian herbs and spices hardly seems like diet food. These mushroom-stuffed zucchini boats make an easy and impressive dish that is low in calories but still filling. Serve with a piece of fish, or serve alone for lunch.

- 2 tablespoons olive oil
- 2 cups button mushrooms, finely chopped
- 2 cloves garlic, finely chopped
- 2 tablespoons chicken broth
- 1 tablespoon flat-leaf parsley, finely chopped
- 1 tablespoon Italian seasoning
- Sea salt and freshly ground pepper, to taste
- 2 medium zucchini, cut in half lengthwise

Preheat oven to 350 degrees.

Heat a large skillet over medium heat, and add the olive oil.

Add the mushrooms and cook until tender, about 4 minutes.

Add the garlic and cook for 2 more minutes.

Add the chicken broth and cook another 3–4 minutes.

Add the parsley and Italian seasoning, and season with sea salt and freshly ground pepper.

Stir and remove from heat.

Scoop out the insides of the halved zucchini and stuff with mushroom mixture.

Place zucchini in a casserole dish, and drizzle a tablespoon of water or broth in the bottom.

Cover with foil and bake for 30–40 minutes until zucchini are tender.

Serve immediately.

Serves 2.

Roasted Balsamic Brussels Sprouts with Pecans

This is a terrific recipe for those who say they don't like Brussels sprouts, as roasting them brings out their sweetness. The vinegar helps by adding a tart flavor as well, and will make getting your daily requirement of vegetables a breeze. Substitute walnuts or almonds for the pecans, if you prefer.

- 20–25 medium-sized Brussels sprouts, quartered
- 2 tablespoons olive oil
- 1 tablespoon balsamic vinegar
- Sea salt and freshly ground pepper, to taste
- 1/4 cup chopped pecans, toasted

Preheat oven to 400 degrees.

Spread sprouts on a single layer on a baking sheet.

Drizzle with olive oil, vinegar, sea salt, and freshly ground pepper.

Roast for 15–20 minutes until tender and caramelized.

Top with the toasted pecans and serve.

Serves 4.

Roasted Beets with Oranges and Onions

When combined with the oranges in this dish, roasted beets become extra sweet and special. Beets are a great source of phytonutrients, so finding more ways to enjoy them will also boost your health. For a hearty lunch, top the salad with crumbled feta or goat cheese.

- 4 medium beets, trimmed and scrubbed
- Juice and zest of 2 oranges
- 1 red onion, thinly sliced
- 2 tablespoons olive oil
- 1 tablespoon red wine vinegar
- Juice of 1 lemon
- Sea salt and freshly ground pepper, to taste

Preheat oven to 400 degrees.

Wrap the beets in a foil pack and close tightly. Place them on a baking sheet and roast 40 minutes until tender enough to be pierced easily with a knife.

Cool until easy to handle.

Combine the beets with the orange juice and zest, red onion, olive oil, vinegar, and lemon juice.

Season with sea salt and freshly ground pepper to taste, and toss lightly.

Allow to sit for about 15 minutes for the flavors to meld before serving.

Serves 6.

Rosemary-Roasted Acorn Squash

When roasted at high heat, the skin of acorn squash becomes soft, tender, and edible. Meanwhile, the benefits of rosemary are many: it is thought to stimulate the immune system, increase circulation, and improve digestion.

- 1 acorn squash
- 2 tablespoons honey
- 2 tablespoons rosemary, finely chopped
- 2 tablespoons olive oil
- Sea salt, to taste

Preheat oven to 400 degrees.

Cut squash in half, and clean out the seeds.

Slice each half into 4 wedges.

Mix honey, rosemary, and olive oil.

Lay squash on baking sheet, and sprinkle each slice with a bit of the mixture and a touch of sea salt.

Turn over and sprinkle other side.

Bake for 30 minutes or so until squash is tender and slightly caramelized, turning each slice over halfway through.

Serve immediately.

Serves 4.

Sautéed Crunchy Greens

If you're looking for a super-low-calorie dish, you can't go wrong with greens. There is no other food that is as low calorie and nutrient dense, so enjoy! Plus, the sunflower seeds included in this dish are high in vitamins B1 and E, manganese, copper, tryptophan, magnesium, selenium, and more.

- 3 tablespoons olive oil
- 2 cloves garlic, minced
- 2 large bunches Swiss chard or kale, sliced, stems removed
- Juice of 1/2 lemon
- Sea salt and freshly ground pepper, to taste
- 3 tablespoons sunflower seeds

In a large skillet, heat the olive oil, and add the garlic on medium heat.

Sauté for about a minute, and add the Swiss chard.

Cook until wilted, about 2 more minutes.

Add the lemon juice, sea salt and freshly ground pepper to taste, and sunflower seeds.

Serve and enjoy!

Serves 4.

Sautéed Mustard Greens and Red Peppers

Greens are considered to be one of the keys to the longevity of the inhabitants of Crete. Sautéing them and flavoring them simply will add to your enjoyment of eating them. Add a pinch of red chili flakes if you want a bit more spice in this scrumptious veggie delight.

- 1 tablespoon olive oil
- 1/2 red pepper, diced
- 2 cloves garlic, minced
- 1 bunch mustard greens
- Sea salt and freshly ground pepper, to taste
- 1 teaspoon white wine vinegar

Heat olive oil in a large saucepan over medium heat. Add bell pepper and garlic, and sauté for 1 minute, stirring often.

Add greens to pan and immediately cover to begin steaming. Set a timer for 2 minutes.

After 1 minute, lift lid and stir greens well, then immediately put lid back on for remaining minute. Remove the lid, season with sea salt and freshly ground pepper, sprinkle with vinegar, and serve.

Serves 4.

Stuffed Bell Peppers

Red bell peppers have more nutrients than green or yellow peppers, including plenty of vitamin C and carotenoids, and their nutritional value is best when they are not subjected to high heat. If you've already had your dairy allowance for the day, simply omit the cheese.

- 3/4 cup feta cheese
- 1/2 cup low-salt olives, pitted
- 1/2 cup plain Greek yogurt
- 1/4 cup minced onion
- 1/4 cup olive oil
- 1 teaspoon thyme, finely chopped
- 1/2 teaspoon dried dill weed
- 6 bell peppers, seeded, cored, and cut in half lengthwise

Combine all the ingredients except the bell peppers in a food processor.

Pulse for 30 seconds, or until blended.

Carefully spoon the mixture into the bell peppers.

Refrigerate for up to 4 hours. Drizzle with olive oil before serving.

Serves 6.

Stuffed Cucumbers

Cucumbers contain a lot of water and also have antioxidant and anti-inflammatory properties. This juicy summer treat makes a great side dish or snack.

- 1 English cucumber
- 1 tomato, diced
- 1 avocado, diced
- Dash of lime juice
- Sea salt and freshly ground pepper, to taste
- Small bunch cilantro, chopped

Cut the cucumber in half lengthwise and scoop out the flesh and seeds into a small bowl.

Without mashing too much, gently combine the cucumber flesh and seeds with the tomato, avocado, and lime juice.

Season with sea salt and freshly ground pepper to taste.

Put mixture back into cucumber halves and cut each piece in half.

Garnish with the cilantro and serve.

Serves 2.

Swiss Chard with White Beans and Bell Peppers

Greens and beans are traditionally paired together in Italian cuisine. Beans are cheap, nutritional powerhouses that fill you up. Use a red bell pepper whenever possible in recipes that call for bell peppers; they are riper and have more nutrients.

- 2 tablespoons olive oil
- 1 medium onion, chopped
- 1 bell pepper, diced
- 2 cloves garlic, minced
- 1 large bunch of Swiss chard, tough stems removed, cut into bite-size pieces
- 2 cups white beans, cooked
- Sea salt and freshly ground pepper, to taste

Heat the oil in a large skillet over medium-high heat. Add the onion and pepper and cook for 5 minutes until soft.

Add the garlic, stir, and add the Swiss chard. Cook for 10 minutes until greens are tender.

Add the beans, stir until heated through, and season with sea salt and freshly ground pepper.

Serve immediately.

Serves 4.

Vibrant Green Beans

These green beans make a delicious addition to roasted meats and are a great alternative to bland, green bean dishes. If you prefer, use lemon juice in place of the wine. Whenever possible, use fresh green beans.

- 2 tablespoons olive oil
- 2 leeks, white parts only, sliced
- Sea salt and freshly ground pepper, to taste
- 1 pound fresh green string beans, trimmed
- 1 tablespoon Italian seasoning
- 2 tablespoons white wine
- Zest of 1 lemon

Heat the olive oil over medium heat in a large skillet.

Add leeks and cook, stirring often, until they start to brown and become lightly caramelized.

Season with sea salt and freshly ground pepper.

Add green beans and Italian seasoning, cooking for a few minutes until beans are tender but still crisp to the bite.

Add the wine and continue cooking until beans are done to your liking and leeks are crispy and browned.

Sprinkle with lemon zest before serving.

Serves 6.

(12)

DESSERTS

- Balsamic Strawberries
- Banana Cream Pie Parfaits
- Berry Crumble
- Cocoa and Coconut Banana Slices
- Cranberry-Orange Cheesecake Pears
- Cucumber-Lime Popsicles
- Fresh Figs with Chocolate Sauce
- Frozen Raspberry Delight
- Grilled Stone Fruit
- Honey-Vanilla Apple Pie with Olive Oil Crust
- Orange and Whipped-Cheese Dessert Cups
- Pears with Blue Cheese and Walnuts
- Red-Wine Poached Pears

Balsamic Strawberries

Strawberries with balsamic vinegar is a classic Italian treat. This easy and unique way to eat fresh summer berries even works if the berries are not as flavorful as you might like. Allow the berries to macerate for a few minutes before serving.

- 2 cups strawberries, hulled and sliced
- 2 tablespoons sugar
- 2 tablespoons balsamic vinegar

Put the strawberries in a bowl, sprinkle with the sugar, and lightly drizzle with the balsamic vinegar.

Toss to combine and let sit for about 10 minutes before serving.

Serves 2.

Banana Cream Pie Parfaits

Low-fat vanilla pudding and graham cracker crumbs make this a simple and healthful treat, with walnuts and bananas providing potassium and omega-3 fatty acids. These parfaits can be prepared ahead of time, making this an easy dessert option for a picnic.

- 1 cup nonfat vanilla pudding
- 2 low-sugar graham crackers, crushed
- 1 banana, peeled and sliced
- 1/4 cup walnuts, chopped
- Honey for drizzling

In small parfait dishes or glasses, layer the ingredients, starting with the pudding and ending with chopped walnuts.

You can repeat the layers, depending on the size of the glass and your preferences.

Drizzle with the honey.

Serve chilled.

Serves 2.

Berry Crumble

While this may seem like a decadent dessert, it's actually loaded with antioxidant-filled berries and cholesterol-lowering oats. If you don't have a cast-iron skillet, simply use a casserole dish instead. Use naturally sweet, ripe berries in this easy-to-make dessert.

• 3 cups frozen, mixed berries	• 1 tablespoon whole-wheat flour
• 1 cup rolled oats	
• 2 tablespoons brown sugar	• 2 tablespoons margarine

Preheat oven to 400 degrees.

In a 10-inch cast-iron skillet, lay the berries in an even layer.

Mix the oats with the sugar and flour in a large mixing bowl.

Spread the oat mixture evenly on top of the berries.

Crumble with the butter, and bake for 40–50 minutes until top is brown and berries are bubbly.

Serve warm.

Serves 6.

Cocoa and Coconut Banana Slices

Frozen bananas have a creamy consistency that mimics ice cream. Bananas are good for you, too—providing dietary fiber, vitamin C, potassium, and manganese. This dessert makes a great snack for adults and kids alike.

- 1 banana, peeled and sliced
- 2 tablespoons unsweetened, shredded coconut
- 1 tablespoon unsweetened cocoa powder
- 1 teaspoon honey

Lay the banana slices on a parchment-lined baking sheet in a single layer.

Put in the freezer for about 10 minutes, until firm but not frozen solid.

Mix the coconut with the cocoa powder in a small bowl.

Roll the banana slices in honey, followed by the coconut mixture.

You can either eat immediately or put back in the freezer for a frozen, sweet treat.

Serves 1.

Cranberry-Orange Cheesecake Pears

For this fruity, creamy treat, use the lightest cream cheese you can find, or substitute low- or nonfat ricotta. On the other hand, pears are very nutritious, a good source of fiber, and low in calories. Finally, the cranberries and almonds add flavor but can be swapped out for other dried fruit and nuts, if you prefer.

- 5 firm pears
- 1 cup unsweetened cranberry juice
- 1 cup freshly squeezed orange juice
- 1 tablespoon pure vanilla extract
- 1/2 teaspoon ground cinnamon
- 1/2 cup low-fat cream cheese, softened
- 1/4 teaspoon ground ginger
- 1/4 teaspoon almond extract
- 1/4 cup dried, unsweetened cranberries
- 1/4 cup sliced almonds, toasted

Peel the pears and slice off the bottoms so they sit upright.

Remove the inside cores, and put the pears in a wide saucepan.

Add the cranberry and orange juice, as well as the vanilla and cinnamon extract.

Bring to a boil, and reduce to a simmer.

Cover and simmer on low heat for 25–30 minutes, until pears are soft but not falling apart.

Beat the cream cheese with the ginger and almond extract.

Stir the cranberries and almonds into the cream cheese mixture.

Once the pears have cooled, spoon the cream cheese into them.

Boil the remaining juices down to a syrup, and drizzle over the top of the filled pears.

Serves 5.

Cucumber-Lime Popsicles

Cucumbers have both antioxidant and anti-inflammatory properties, and adults and kids alike love these easy-to-make summer treats.

- 2 cups cold water
- 1 cucumber, peeled
- 1/4 cup honey
- Juice of 1 lime

In a blender, puree the water, cucumber, honey, and lime juice.

Pour into popsicle molds, freeze, and enjoy on a hot summer day!

Serves 4–6.

Fresh Figs with Chocolate Sauce

Desserts in the Mediterranean are simple and often fruity. This easy treat would be a good snack, too. You could also serve it with Greek yogurt.

- 1/4 cup honey
- 2 tablespoons cocoa powder
- 8 fresh figs

Combine the honey and cocoa powder in a small bowl, and mix well to form a syrup.

Cut the figs in half and place cut side up.

Drizzle with the syrup and serve.

Serves 4.

Frozen Raspberry Delight

You can make a sorbet-style treat with frozen fruit. While truly tasty, this dessert will also help you meet your daily fruit requirement. Swap the peach or mango for a banana, if you prefer.

- 3 cups frozen raspberries
- 1 peach, peeled and pitted
- 1 mango, peeled and pitted
- 1 teaspoon honey

Add all ingredients to a blender and puree, only adding enough water to keep the mixture moving and your blender from overworking itself.

Freeze for 10 minutes to firm up if desired.

Serves 2.

Grilled Stone Fruit

Juicy summer fruit provides hydration in addition to vitamins. These stone fruits are also delicious drizzled with balsamic vinegar instead of cheese and honey for a savory side dish.

- 2 peaches, halved and pitted
- 2 plums, halved and pitted
- 3 apricots, halved and pitted
- 1/2 cup low-fat ricotta cheese
- 2 tablespoons honey

Heat grill to medium heat.

Oil the grates or spray with cooking spray.

Place the fruit cut side down on the grill, and grill for 2–3 minutes per side, until lightly charred and soft.

Serve warm with the ricotta and drizzle with honey.

Serves 2.

Honey-Vanilla Apple Pie with Olive Oil Crust

Olive oil is the preferred cooking oil on the Mediterranean diet and can be used successfully in baking. The whole-wheat flour will give the pie a rustic appearance.

For the crust:
- 1/4 cup olive oil
- 1 1/2 cups whole-wheat flour
- 1/2 teaspoon sea salt
- 2 tablespoons ice water

For the filling:
- 4 large apples of your choice, peeled, cored, and sliced
- Juice of 1 lemon
- 1 tablespoon pure vanilla extract
- 1 tablespoon honey
- 1/2 teaspoon sea salt
- Olive oil

Make the crust:

Put the olive oil, flour, and sea salt in a food processor and process until dough forms.

Slowly add the water and pulse until you have a stiff dough.

Form the dough into 2 equal-sized balls, wrap in plastic wrap, and put in the refrigerator while you make the filling.

Make the filling:

Combine the apples, lemon juice, vanilla, honey, and sea salt in a large bowl.

Stir and allow to sit for at least 10 minutes.

Preheat oven to 400 degrees.

Roll 1 crust out on a lightly floured surface. Transfer to a 9-inch pie plate and top with filling.

Roll the other ball of dough out and put on top of the pie. Cut a few slices in the top to vent the pie, and lightly brush the top of the pie with olive oil.

Bake for 45 minutes, or until top is browned and apples are bubbly.

Allow to cool completely before slicing and serving with your favorite frozen yogurt.

Serves 8.

Orange and Whipped-Cheese Dessert Cups

Although this dessert is very simple to make, it tastes decadent and is pretty to look at. This makes it a great dessert to serve to guests or after a romantic dinner for two. The taste is similar to cheesecake, but with a creamier texture and a good deal less sugar.

- 1 cup part-skim ricotta cheese
- 1 cup low-fat cream cheese
- 2 tablespoons honey
- 2 tablespoons low-fat milk
- 1/2 teaspoon vanilla
- 1/2 teaspoon cinnamon
- 2 teaspoons honey
- 1/2 teaspoon allspice
- 1/4 teaspoon nutmeg
- 3 large navel oranges, sectioned with membrane removed
- Fresh basil leaves for garnish

In a blender or food processor, combine the ricotta, cream cheese, honey, milk, vanilla, and cinnamon and process until smooth.

Spoon into 4 dessert cups, cover and refrigerate.

In a medium heavy skillet, heat the honey until thin and warm. Stir in the allspice and nutmeg until well mixed.

Add the orange slices and cook for 1 minute. Gently turn the orange slices over and cook for 1–2 minutes or until just beginning to brown. Remove from heat.

Allow the orange slices to cool to room temperature, then top each dessert dish with 1/4 of the oranges. To serve, garnish with a basil leaf.

Serves 4.

Pears with Blue Cheese and Walnuts

Fruit, cheese, and nuts are a classic combination, regarding flavor but also health—walnuts provide a good source of omega-3 fatty acids, and pears are a good source of fiber. Enjoy this treat as a dessert or healthful snack.

- 1–2 pears, cored and sliced into 12 slices
- 1/4 cup blue cheese crumbles
- 12 walnut halves
- 1 tablespoon honey

Lay the pear slices on a plate, and top with the blue cheese crumbles.

Top each slice with 1 walnut, and drizzle with honey.

Serve and enjoy!

Serves 1.

Red-Wine Poached Pears

Red wine is encouraged on this diet and is popular with meals in Italy, France, and Spain. Pears are a low-calorie fruit and a good source of fiber. These make a delicious dessert but are also lovely alongside rich meat dishes as well.

- 2 cups red wine, such as Merlot or Zinfandel, more if necessary
- 2 firm pears, peeled
- 2–3 cardamom pods, split
- 1 cinnamon stick
- 2 peppercorns
- 1 bay leaf

Put all ingredients in a large pot and bring to a boil.

Make sure the pears are submerged in the wine.

Reduce heat and simmer for 15–20 minutes until the pears are tender when poked with a fork.

Remove the pears from the wine, and allow to cool.

Bring the wine to a boil, and cook until it reduces to a syrup.

Strain and drizzle the pears with the warmed syrup before serving.

Serves 2.